Universal Periodic Review of Human Rights

Towards Best Practice

Edited by Dr Purna Sen
Research by Monica Vincent

COMMONWEALTH SECRETARIAT

Commonwealth Secretariat
Marlborough House, Pall Mall
London SW1Y 5HX
United Kingdom

Published by the Commonwealth Secretariat

The Human Rights Unit would like to thank Jade Cochran for her additional research in the preparation of this publication

Edited and designed by Wayzgoose
Cover design by Michael Orton Designs
Cover photo credit: UN Photo
Printed by Hobbs the Printers Ltd, Totton, Hampshire

Views and opinions expressed in this publication are the responsibility of the authors and should in no way be attributed to the institutions to which they are affiliated or to the Commonwealth Secretariat.

Wherever possible, the Commonwealth Secretariat uses paper sourced from sustainable forests or from sources that minimise a destructive impact on the environment.

Copies of this publication may be obtained from

The Publications Section
Commonwealth Secretariat
Marlborough House, Pall Mall
London SW1Y 5HX
United Kingdom
Tel: +44 (0)20 7747 6534
Fax: +44 (0)20 7839 9081
Email: publications@commonwealth.int
Web: www.thecommonwealth.org/publications

A catalogue record for this publication is available from the British Library.

ISBN: 978-1-84929-005-0 (paperback)
ISBN: 978-1-84959-041-0 (downloadable e-book)

Contents

Abbreviations

AFSPA	Armed Forces Special Powers Act (India)
APF	Asia Pacific Forum of National Human Rights Institutions
CAT	Convention Against Torture and Other Cruel, Inhuman or Degrading Treatment or Punishment
CEDAW	Convention on the Elimination of all Forms of Discrimination Against Women
CHRAJ	Commission on Human Rights and Administrative Justice (Ghana)
CHRI	Commonwealth Human Rights Initiative
CID	Criminal Investigation Department (South Africa)
CRC	Convention on the Rights of the Child
CRPD	Convention on the Rights of Persons with Disabilities
CSO	civil society organisation
ECPT	European Convention for the Prevention of Torture
EJEs	extra judicial executions
ESCR	economic, social and cultural rights
FCO	Foreign and Commonwealth Office (UK)
FoE	freedom of expression
HRC	Human Rights Council
HRD	human rights defender
HRU	Human Rights Unit
ICC	International Coordinating Committee of National Human Rights Institutions
ICCPR	International Covenant on Civil and Political Rights
ICESCR	International Covenant on Economic, Social and Cultural Rights
IDPs	internally displaced persons
INGO	international non-governmental organisation
MoJ	Ministry of Justice (UK)
MWC	International Convention on the Protection of the Rights of All Migrant Workers and Members of their Families
NAP	national action plan
NGO	non-governmental organisation
NHRI	national human rights institution
OHCHR	Office of the High Commissioner for Human Rights
SuR	state under review
UK	United Kingdom of Great Britain and Northern Ireland
UN	United Nations

UNDP	United Nations Development Programme
UNHCHR	United Nations High Commissioner for Human Rights
UPR	Universal Periodic Review

Preface

The Universal Periodic Review of the United Nations Human Rights Council enjoys the full support of the Commonwealth. Designed to ensure equal treatment for every country, it allows countries to show how they are fulfilling their human rights obligations.

The UPR is not just about being reviewed by the Human Rights Council in Geneva. It is about progressing, promoting and protecting human rights on the ground. It is at the follow-up stage – the actual implementation of the recommendations accepted by the states – that it brings about meaningful change.

The Commonwealth Secretariat's Human Rights Unit has organised a series of seminars for all Commonwealth member states reporting under the UPR process. These seminars are true to the three-way spirit of partnership in the UPR, in which governments, national human rights institutions or ombudsman's offices and civil society organisations all participate together. This approach has been a vehicle for important cross-country conversation, as well as detailed learning and sharing.

The Commonwealth will continue to support the UPR. This type of assistance is instrumental in advancing human rights – one of the fundamental values of the Commonwealth.

I warmly commend this publication.

Kamalesh Sharma
Commonwealth Secretary-General
London, June 2009

Foreword

The United Nations Office of the High Commissioner for Human Rights (OHCHR) welcomes its co-operation with the Commonwealth Secretariat and its Human Rights Unit, which is fully engaged in sharing experiences and assisting the Commonwealth's 53 member states on human rights issues and in raising awareness of international human rights standards, mechanisms and procedures, and of recent developments in this field.

A new challenge emerged with the establishment of the UN Human Rights Council (HRC) and the creation of its Universal Periodic Review (UPR). The UPR uniquely provides for a review of human rights in all 192 UN member states over a four year period (2008–2011). With the adoption of the four-year timetable member states agreed to the order of the review. While the UPR was an unfamiliar process, it has been established that it is a co-operative mechanism that reviews, on an equal basis, the promotion and protection of human rights in all UN member states. Despite the novelty of the UPR procedure, concerned member states have all appeared before the HRC's UPR working group for review and before its plenary for the adoption of the outcome of that review.

This publication represents an additional contribution to improving understanding and knowledge of the UPR. Contributors have been selected from the different stakeholders in the UPR process, including representatives of states, national human rights institutions (NHRIs), non-governmental organisations (NGOs) and civil society. Their practical experiences and their different perspectives on the UPR will help to explain its significance both as a mechanism and process: from the preparation of reports to the review in Geneva and the implementation of the recommendations made to states and their commitments to follow them up. In reality, the UPR is increasingly being perceived as an evolving process. We have much to learn from the examples shared in this publication about the opportunities for the various stakeholders to work with states on follow-up.

We should not forget that the UPR is just one year old and that two-thirds of UN member states are still to be reviewed under the first round. This publication can play a useful role in the continuous appraisal and evaluation of the effectiveness of the UPR, as a formal assessment of the mechanism will take place in the Human Rights Council in 2011, before the second round of the UPR process.

Giuliano Comba
Chief, Universal Periodic Review Section
Office of the High Commissioner for Human Rights

Introduction

The Commonwealth Secretariat is fully committed to supporting both the new universal review process and the active, informed and full participation of states and stakeholders from the Commonwealth. Thanks to financial support from the UK Foreign and Commonwealth Office (FCO), in March 2008 the Secretariat's Human Rights Unit (HRU) began an detailed programme of work that addressed these objectives. The programme has four key elements:

- Sharing technical information about the procedure and modalities;

- Building the capacity and confidence of states in engaging and maximising the outcomes of their engagement in the process;

- Building stakeholder knowledge of, and participation in, the process;

- Learning from states and stakeholders that have been through the Geneva element of the UPR.

These elements have been pursued in a variety of ways: a series of seminars that included both states and stakeholders; observation of Commonwealth state sessions during the UPR process in Geneva; and participation in non-Commonwealth seminars on the UPR. Staff from the UN participated in and supported all the HRU seminars. Their knowledge of the UPR has been a critical part of the information-sharing component and they have readily promoted the HRU's efforts to disseminate information.

This publication draws together important strands of the discussions held during the first year of the UPR, especially in terms of contributions from states and stakeholders and from the UN High Commissioner for Human Rights (UNHCHR). The Secretariat's expertise about the new process has grown during this first year and we are now looked to for advice and input from many quarters, including some that are outside the Commonwealth. In this publication we offer commentary on the process and some initial quantitative analysis of the interactive dialogue and recommendations as experienced by Commonwealth states.

Key messages that emerge from this document are that:

- Many parties, both states and stakeholders, find the new process unfamiliar and confusing;

- This uncertainty did not stand in the way of enthusiasm among states that went through the UPR process in 2008;

- Much goodwill was extended by states under review towards the UPR;

- Some saw the Geneva element as a dialogue and exchange rather than as an examination;

- The states that felt they gained the most were those that treated the UPR as a chance to listen, learn and harness support;

- The first year of the UPR has been a great learning experience;

- Attention must now be paid to follow-up;

- Consultation and co-operation across sectors indicate not only conformity with UPR guidelines, but also good practice in the promotion of human rights;

- There is no one right model for UPR engagement – many are documented herein.

One year into the UPR, this publication compiles experiences, draws together recommendations and considers ways forward that may be able to strengthen the process and bring the UPR home to the peoples of the Commonwealth. These are still early days, but taking stock is always a useful exercise. In 2010, half-way through the UPR cycle, the Human Rights Unit will hold a review meeting. At that point we aim to pull together further experiences to strengthen the shaping of good practice, that has been started but not completed at this point.

I hope that this publication will be of use to those coming to the UPR for the first time – both states and stakeholders – and in the discussions that are now beginning about follow-up. I offer my thanks to those who have contributed to the publication, either by allowing their talks to be edited and published or by writing new pieces. Together we have taken forward the spirit of collaboration embodied in the UPR. I affirm the willingness of the HRU to offer advice and support in the preparation stage for states coming up for the UPR and for stakeholders that will be participating in the process and in the implementation phases.

Dr Purna Sen
Head of Human Rights
Commonwealth Secretariat

Collaborating with the Commonwealth Secretariat

It is a great privilege to be asked to contribute to the Commonwealth Secretariat's publication in the Universal Periodic Review.

The UPR is one of the most important innovations of the United Nations Human Rights Council. That is why we all need to build a review mechanism that is open and transparent, as well as consistent and co-operative. As one of the first countries to be reviewed, the UK aimed to establish a positive precedent. We have approached the process candidly, constructively and co-operatively, and we encourage other states to do the same. In order to ensure that the UPR fulfils its mandate and is a truly universal process, we have participated actively in every review. We have asked questions and made recommendations to every state reviewed so far.

We are delighted to be able to support and participate in the series of seminars that the Secretariat's Human Rights Unit is running to prepare states for their reviews. Because we were reviewed in the first week of the UPR, we hoped that others would find our experience helpful in their own preparations. These seminars have also been enormously helpful to us, as we have gained a wealth of ideas from others and improved our understanding of human rights within the Commonwealth. We hope to continue our fruitful partnership with the Commonwealth Secretariat to offer support to states during the follow-up process and implementation of recommendations.

A key component of a successful UPR process is the involvement of civil society. Civil society played an important part in the preparation of our own review. We are working to encourage other participating governments to take a similar approach and to raise awareness of the UPR process among civil society organisations (CSOs) around the world.

A good review allows countries to take a self-critical look at their own human rights situation, to discuss the challenges they face with peers and take steps to improve the human rights situation in their countries. A successful review is not one in which no criticisms are made; every state has human rights challenges. Ultimately each review is a success if it leads to the country concerned addressing those challenges in co-operation with others, and improving people's lives.

I look forward to sharing our experience with my colleagues in other Commonwealth countries as more of us move towards the implementation phase and the prospect of showing progress in our second reviews.

Susan Hyland
Head of Human Rights, Democracy and Governance Group
Foreign and Commonwealth Office, UK

Introduction to the Universal Periodic Review Process*

Background

The now defunct UN Commission on Human Rights examined and monitored human rights concerns on a selective country-by-country basis. The Commission was discredited by its perceived politicisation, which hindered constructive dialogue on human rights issues. In 2006, the Human Rights Council replaced the Commission and, together with other changes, introduced the new UPR mechanism under Resolution 5/1.[1]

The UPR treats every country equally and it was hoped that the previous controversial approach to country situations and resolutions would be replaced by objective assessments. While country-specific resolutions still exist in the Human Rights Council, the UPR process has meant that all countries' human rights policies and situations are scrutinised and that every state is subject to equal treatment by the international community.

The technical characteristics stipulated in Resolution 5/1 called for a comprehensive process both in relation to member states and to the rights covered by the exercise. A unique feature of the UPR process is the three-dimensional approach wherein a country must make its own self-assessment in a national report and is also reviewed against information contained in the reports of UN treaty bodies, independent experts (known as special procedures) and other UN bodies, as well as information compiled from reports of national human rights institutions (NHRIs) and non-governmental organisations (NGOs). These features make the UPR an unprecedented system of monitoring compliance with human rights obligations.

Why is the UPR mechanism important?

The UPR has much potential because it provides a detailed account of the human rights situation on the ground. To benefit from the UPR exercise, countries should subject themselves to honest and genuine critical self-assessment in evaluating achievements and challenges. The UPR mechanism is not intended to be a self-congratulatory mechanism.

---

*Contributed by Ibrahim Salama, Chief, Human Rights Treaties Branch, Office of the High Commissioner for Human Rights.

The UPR mechanism is also important for encouraging international co-operation, which can help to achieve the mainstreaming of human rights. In this context, the UPR has huge potential for paving the way for a conceptual shift from co-existence to co-operation. For the first time, the UPR brings together the right to criticise and an obligation to co-operate on practical steps to establishing better human rights in a given country.

How to prepare the state report

Resolution 5/1 and the guidelines for the state report[2] emphasise the need for a broad consultative process. An ideal state report should be a genuine depiction of human rights at the national level. The state should also move ahead from the traditional narrative and descriptive style of reporting and instead evaluate both its achievements and its shortcomings. Such a shift in reporting will contribute significantly towards addressing real issues and concerns.

If absolutely necessary, the reports can be oral, but they should cover the following: country background; a human rights vision; an analysis of the situation in terms of achievements, obstacles, intentions and commitments for the future; and expectations with respect to international co-operation.

The national preparatory process guarantees added value to the stakeholders (NHRIs and NGOs) as the UPR process calls for structural and compulsory dialogue at national level. Countries that have a free press and independent civil society will find that the consultative processes will have even greater value.

Weighing up the UPR process

The UPR mechanism has both weak and strong points. The fact that the country undergoing review can determine the issues under discussion, the conduct of operation and even the outcomes of the whole exercise may be a potential weakness of the system. Under the UPR process, member states are at the same time both parties and judges. Although this is inherent in any peer review exercise, it is hoped that bilateral relations will influence debate and that the collegial nature of the exercise will go some way towards meeting this relatively weak point.

Further to the strong attributes mentioned earlier, an outstanding feature is that, for the first time, the process for monitoring and examining human rights by the international community is focused on a bottom-up approach. This is through NHRIs and NGOS providing substantial reference to the realities on the ground through stakeholder reports.

There is much potential for the UPR process to be successful in protecting and promoting human rights – though this depends entirely on how the member states engage and participate in the process. It is certainly an opportunity for all countries – developed and developing, North and South – to be subject to the same treatment. As indicated above, the UPR process has much potential for promoting and protecting human rights on the ground and relies upon the full involvement of states, NHRIs and civil society organisations for the realisation of this potential.

UPR seminar for Commonwealth countries reporting in 2008, Commonwealth Secretariat, London, March 2008.

The Universal Periodic Review as Mechanism and Process*

The Universal Periodic Review is widely perceived to be a tool of the Human Rights Council (HRC), which meets in Geneva. It is indeed that, but that is not all. It is helpful to consider the UPR both as a mechanism and a process. The mechanism is the part that takes place in Geneva and the process is a much larger and longer project that begins before the Geneva element and extends considerably beyond it.

UPR – the mechanism

A set of flow charts that simplify the UPR process are included in this publication (Annex 3), as is Resolution 5/1, which sets out the new mechanism (Annex 1). A brief summary should serve as a straightforward run-through and explanation.

The UPR commits the UN, through the HRC, to review every state's record and the challenges it faces in promoting human rights. The review is by peers, rather than by experts steeped in the law, language and mechanics of human rights. Other mechanisms – special procedures – perform this function, so there is no need to recreate these in the HRC. All 192 UN member states must undergo review under the Geneva-based mechanism, with 48 reviewed each year in three batches of 16 – the sequence having been determined through a random selection process. An HRC working group is convened for the UPR, for two weeks, three times a year. Three documents provide a written basis for the review, together with an oral presentation by the state under review (SuR). The heart of the review is a three-hour session, known as the interactive dialogue, in which the SuR speaks to issues raised in the documents and in which any questions previously put to the state can also be addressed. Members of the HRC and observer states may participate in the dialogue, putting questions, making suggestions or raising issues of concern by putting their names on a list.

The SuR is guided and supported through the process by a group of three other states – known as the troika. These are randomly selected states, although they should in principle include one from the region of the SuR, and very few names have been rejected by any SuR. The troika meets with the SuR before and during the review. Together they discuss the process and the troika feeds through any questions or comments from other states that have been submitted in advance of the interactive dialogue. The troika is available to discuss options and responses to recommendations put to the SuR.

*Contributed by Dr Purna Sen, Head of Human Rights, Commonwealth Secretariat.

The SuR is sovereign in determining which of the suggestions and recommendations made to them they are willing to accept. International standards and norms, recommendations of treaty bodies and other special procedures and other accepted frameworks will together form a strong point of reference for discussions and for anticipated agreement on future work. The UPR is intended to be a review and a collective commitment for action – through the working group discussions other states offer support and advice on the implementation of accepted recommendations. Other organisations, such as the UN, aid agencies and the Commonwealth Secretariat, also make their services and funds available.

The interactive dialogue is followed two days later by the adoption of the report of the dialogue. This document, drawn up by the OHCHR, details the discussions and initial responses of the SuR, as well as recommendations made in the working group. The final step of the mechanism involves consideration of the report of the SuR by the next session of the HRC plenary, at which time the SuR has the opportunity to make a statement and answer questions, and other states can make observations. This is the session at which stakeholders can make oral contributions. This is the point at which the final outcome document of the SuR is adopted; the document includes any voluntary pledges and commitments made by the SuR.

UPR – the process

The flowcharts in Annex 3 refer to two elements that are not Geneva based: the pre- and post-Geneva periods. As described above, the UPR mechanism forms a technical but significant element in a larger project – that of promoting human rights in member states.

It is through reporting and sharing challenges in this endeavour that greater energy and expertise can be galvanised towards collective efforts to realise human rights. Offers of technical support and co-operation can flow from the mechanism to support the process on the ground. The UN has established trust funds (Annex 4) to assist states where resource constraints limit human rights development work. The follow-up phase, as it is now being seen, is closely linked to the Geneva mechanism, as this is where the accepted recommendations and voluntary pledges to action, as well as offers of support, need to be made real. In time, the follow-up phase will become the preparatory phase as the second round of reporting approaches.

The principle of consultation and co-operation between stakeholders and states applies before and after the Geneva element. In some cases this will be a new approach (see the chapter on the experience of a small state in section 2). In others it will be a set of old relationships that will hopefully be refreshed. Not all such relationships are easy or new, yet it remains possible that they can be made to work. Indeed, the UPR may be a useful prompt for the establishment or re-constitution of such relationships. The fact that states have been tasked with under-taking consultation gives them a responsibility; civil society should see this as an opportunity to establish or renew dialogue.

Figure 1. UPR – the process

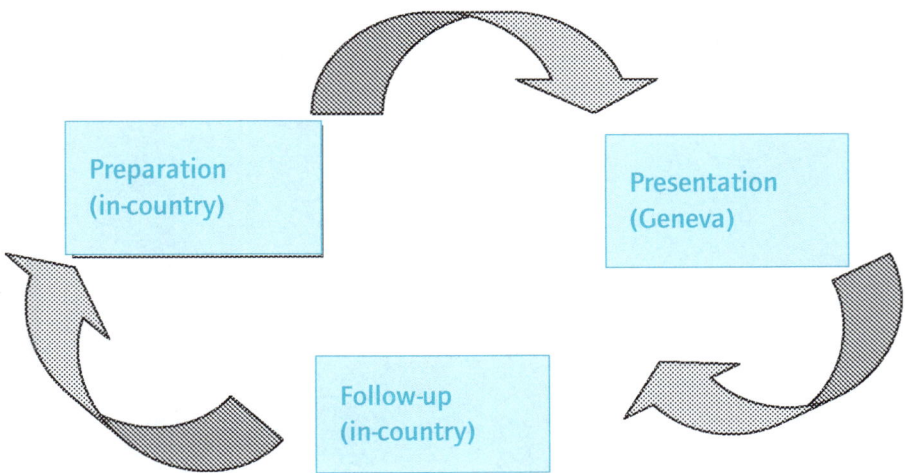

Discussions and consultations within the Commonwealth have acknowledged the difficulties of undertaking a new reporting process: most state departments have not been provided with additional staff for this – nor have NGOs. Moreover, minis-tries tasked with the compilation of state reports have told of the challenges of co-ordinating and compiling information for the UPR. It is helpful to see the UPR as a process, as the relationships built in the compilation stage can be revisited in the follow-up phase. After all, it is likely that implementation will require efforts both from a variety of ministries and from stakeholders.

Delegates at the UPR seminar for Commonwealth Caribbean countries, Barbados, October 2008.

Section I

HOW THE UNIVERSAL PERIODIC REVIEW WORKS

How the UPR Works for States*

The United Kingdom perceives the UPR as a process that encourages equals to come together for a human rights dialogue, and to discuss difficulties faced by states and how best to overcome them. In other words, the approach of the UK to the UPR process concentrates more on dialogue and less on examination.

In the UK, the Ministry of Justice (MoJ) has overall policy responsibility for the development of human rights and for ensuring that the state is fulfilling its international treaty obligations. Further, as the MoJ is responsible for reflecting the outcomes of the UPR process in policies at national level, it was agreed at the outset that the MoJ's Human Rights Department would spearhead the UPR reporting process. Although the onus of preparing the reporting process rested with the MoJ, colleagues from across all government departments supported, participated in and contributed to the briefings on human rights related subjects that would be addressed at the review in Geneva.

The preparatory stages of the report writing were highly demanding as the UPR process was new, the parameters relatively undefined (in comparison with the treaty bodies), questions could be raised from any dimension and there was a broad spectrum of human rights issues to be captured within a tight deadline.

The guidelines to report writing prepared by the OHCHR provided an excellent architecture on how to draft a country report in 20 pages. In the preparation of the report, a country can adapt different approaches. For instance, a country can use its respective UN core documents, including periodic reports submitted to treaty body mechanisms, as its source of information; conversely, the report could feed into the process of updating the UN core documents of the country. Although it is an extra burden, it is not an entirely new type of activity.

The preparation of the UK report was carried out in different stages. As a first step, a ministerial meeting was convened to deliberate on the issues, concerns and possible methods of approaching the UPR reporting process. It was agreed that a state report should acknowledge and reflect genuine issues and challenges, as well as the positive and realistic efforts taken by the state in addressing human rights concerns.

The overriding position was to ensure free and fair consultation with the stakeholders, including NHRIs and CSOs, as referred to in the UPR guidelines. The govern-

---

*From the perspective of the United Kingdom.
Contributed by John Kissane, Deputy Head of the Human Rights Division, Ministry of Justice, UK.

ment was committed to wider consultations and a preliminary meeting with the stakeholders was therefore convened. An outline of the report and the significance of the consultative process was emphasised at this meeting. The meeting was well attended and there was a productive discussion; the outcomes were both critical and constructive. The stakeholders' participation brought to light many human rights issues that required

The UK considers the UPR to be an important innovation and a definite means of improving human rights across the world.

added emphasis. At a later stage, the draft report was circulated to the stakeholders – in good faith that they would not disclose it to the media – for their final comments and suggestions. The consultations and the engagement with the stakeholders proved to be very productive and the UK is committed to continuing this exercise.

As the report was a public document, the editorial task included winning acceptance and approval from colleagues across all government departments. The state report covers human rights issues that are of significance to the UK government.

The UK was keen to have high-level representation for the presentation of the report in Geneva and therefore ministerial representation was sought. On receiving clearance from all government departments, the MoJ was briefed on the task of introducing and presenting the report at the Human Rights Council. The Minister of Justice was open to answering questions raised during the interactive dialogue of the UPR working group session. Twenty-five recommendations were submitted. Of these, 15 were accepted in full, four were partly accepted, five were rejected and one was a question not pertaining to human rights. The UK is currently working on the next steps regarding the implementation of the 15 accepted recommendations.

The UK considers the UPR to be an important innovation and a definite means of improving human rights across the world. The spirit of the UPR is to encourage dialogue and not to be an examination. There are no right or wrong answers. Instead, the UPR promotes conversation between peers on prevailing human rights issues and how these can be taken forward. These dimensions of the process can be attributed to the success of the UPR.

How the UPR Works for National Human Rights Institutions*

In 2008, the UPR process was new and the Commission on Human Rights and Administrative Justice (CHRAJ) felt that there was a lack of clarity and understanding on how to approach this unfamiliar mechanism. On receiving the UPR guidelines and documents from the Human Rights Council, the CHRAJ approached the Ministry of Justice and Attorney General's Department for joint collaboration in the UPR process. The call (from the CHRAJ and the Commonwealth Human Rights Initiative (CHRI),[3] a civil society organisation) for state departments to afford broad consultation with NHRIs and CSOs received no response, as there was ambiguity about the deadlines for submission of the UPR reports.

As the stakeholders' groups (namely NHRIs and CSOs) had relatively shorter timescales for transmitting their submissions to the HRC, the CHRAJ prepared a concise report which was sent to the Ministry of Justice for its comments before submission to the OHCHR.

As the deadline for the national state report for the UPR process approached, the Ministry of Justice called for broad consultation. An inter-ministerial committee, including the Ministries of Justice, Foreign Affairs, Women and Children, Manpower, Youth and Employment, Education, Science and Sports, and Finance and Economic Planning, was called to participate in and contribute towards preparing the report. The government asked the CHRAJ, as well as officials from the police and prison departments, the Ghana Bar Association, the Journalists Association and CSOs, to provide input and assist in the preparation of the report. A number of formal and informal consultations and review workshops were organised to identify key human rights issues, concerns, achievements and challenges. The Ministry of Justice conflated the different contributions and was responsible for drafting, finalising and submitting the report to OHCHR.

The Ghana mission in Geneva was instrumental in providing essential updates and insights into the UPR working group sessions in Geneva. The mission provided useful pointers on many issues, including the size, composition and level of delegations, the presentation of the report by the state under review and how to address the questions raised during the interactive dialogue.

---

*From the perspective of Ghana's NHRI.
Contributed by Anna Bossman, Acting Chairperson of the Commission on Human Rights and Administrative Justice.

The review of Ghana in Geneva included a presentation by the Minister of Justice and the Minister of State for Education. Forty-four countries participated in the interactive dialogue by raising questions and seeking clarifications. Out of the 30 recommendations made, Ghana accepted 22 and rejected six. Some of the recommendations focused on ratification of international human rights treaties, addressing discrimination against women and children, strengthening the capacities of the CHRAJ through increasing funding and resources, and adopting necessary measures including awareness-raising campaigns against harmful traditional practices and stereotypes.

... a high level of collaboration and co-operation with government is essential to produce an effective report.

The CHRAJ is keen to advance and strengthen the UPR process. One of its strategies is to include the recommendations and commitments accepted by the Government into its annual report on human rights in Ghana. Other strategies the CHRAJ will adopt to strengthen the UPR's potential to promote and protect human rights in Ghana are to share information on the UPR process with the NGO forum that is convened on a quarterly basis, to intensify campaigns calling for ratification of various international treaties and to promote human rights legislation.

In the experience of the CHRAJ, a high level of collaboration and co-operation with government is essential to produce an effective report. In addition, information sharing and collaboration with the CSOs and the NHRI is essential to ensure a good understanding of the UPR process. Communication with the mission in Geneva should be used as a helpful resource to keep abreast with the trends at the HRC.

From an NHRI's perspective, the positive aspects of the UPR process are in the opportunities to engage with government before and after the review in Geneva. This involves encouraging national implementation of the commitments made and

assisting with the follow-up before the next round of the UPR in four years time.

How the UPR Works for Non-governmental Organisations*

Background

The Commonwealth Human Rights Initiative (CHRI) made six submissions to the UPR process in 2008. The submissions focused on countries where the CHRI has ongoing projects, where it has sufficient secondary data to prepare reports and where there are constraints on other CSO partners in making submissions to the Human Rights Council.

The information used for the CHRI submissions was gathered through programmes organised in conjunction with national and community level CSOs, from monitoring the news for human rights concerns and from the CHRI's own human rights related analysis undertaken on a thematic basis. The information pooled from these sources was combined to identify important and outstanding human rights issues and concerns which were then verified in consultation with partner organisations.

Experience of the UPR process

The CHRI is supportive of CSOs holding joint consultative meetings and encourages CSOs to arrive at one consolidated submission to transmit to the HRC. This approach encourages consensus on human rights issues, thus avoiding duplication of information and multiple submissions to the OHCHR. The CHRI participated in two such consultations – in India and Ghana.

As called for in Resolution 5/1, the CHRI would like to emphasise the need for and value of states conducting national consultations with stakeholders, including CSOs, when preparing for their national report. CSOs could be of great assistance and may be able to make focused submissions if national consultations are held in advance.

The CHRI calls upon states to follow a planned and transparent process when they are preparing their reports; this helps CSOs to assist in and contribute to a state's national report. Further, as the preparatory stage to UPR is often intense and spread across different ministerial departments, appointing a designated focal person within government helps CSOs in approaching the correct channels when preparing reports and during the follow-up of the recommendations.

---

*From the perspective of the Commonwealth Human Rights Initiative.
Contributed by Uttara Sahani and Iniyan Ilango.

A challenge faced by the CHRI when drafting its submissions relates to the fact that the CHRI's work mainly relates to civil and political rights, whereas the spectrum of human rights is much wider. To ensure that the most pertinent human rights issues – civil, political, economic, social and cultural – are addressed, priority was given to the issues that received

The CHRI calls upon states to follow a planned and transparent process when they are preparing their reports.

most emphasis in the CSO consultations, issues raised by countries in their pledges to the HRC and issues surfacing in the national media as being of national importance.

Recommendations

Following its experience from the first year of the UPR, the CHRI would like to make the following recommendations:

- Commonwealth governments should follow and publish a well-defined timeline for a dedicated, transparent and inclusive consultative process. Co-ordination of the UPR process is essential so that both states and CSOs work in good faith on the preparation of balanced and focused reports.

- Commonwealth governments should streamline their internal processes governing the UPR process. Given the commonalities in institutional and administrative systems, Commonwealth governments could work together to evolve Commonwealth best practices in the area of the UPR.

- Commonwealth governments should keep an up-to-date directory containing contact details of government officials and departments in charge of UPR processes. This will assist both government channels and Commonwealth CSOs in accessing information and in sharing experiences and best practice.

- Commonwealth governments should hold early CSO consultations before the CSO's own UPR submission deadlines. It is suggested that such consultations should not be a one-off event, but rather a continuous process. This would help CSOs in understanding the UPR process and the government's plans and processes in the UPR preparatory work.

- Commonwealth CSOs should assist in the formulation of model guidelines and best practices for approaching the UPR. The CHRI sees the Commonwealth Model National Plan of Action on Human Rights[4] as complementary to this process and strongly encourages its use.

Delegates at the UPR seminar for Commonwealth Caribbean countries,, Barbados, October 2008.

Section II

WHAT HAS BEEN LEARNED?

The Commonwealth Secretariat*

The first year of the UPR

The first year of the new review process has been one of some uncertainty, lack of familiarity, learning, frankness, defensiveness, hope, optimism, relief and much more. As was to be expected, the process has not been without difficulties, but it was by no means a failure. On the contrary, there have been substantive and positive developments and the whole process has been more successful than some expected.

There was understandable scepticism[5] from several quarters before the UPR started and in its very early days there was suspicion that powerful countries would somehow avoid a meaningful critique and that the 'usual suspects' would be the focus of attention. The legacy of the defunct Commission was strong indeed. Informal conversations with many stakeholders suggest strongly that much of the scepticism has dissipated. The potential of the UPR seems to be coming through and goodwill and commitment to the process is growing. This bodes well for the future success of the UPR.

Twelve Commonwealth countries underwent the Geneva element of the UPR in 2008: The Bahamas, Barbados, Botswana, Ghana, India, Pakistan, South Africa, Sri Lanka, Tonga, Tuvalu, UK and Zambia. Their domestic contexts, challenges and successes are diverse: some have been involved in negotiations that have given birth to and shaped the UPR; others do not have missions in Geneva and were unfamiliar with both the HRC and the UPR. This is a considerable disadvantage and small states with resource constraints have keenly felt the challenges of participation and familiarity.

The following chapters focus on lessons to be learned from the first year of the UPR and have been contributed by a small state, an NHRI umbrella organisation and an NGO.

*Contributed by Dr Purna Sen, Head of Human Rights at the Commonwealth Secretariat.

The Experience of a Small State[*]

The UPR mechanism received attention and sanction at the highest level of government in Tonga and the Tongan Foreign Service was keen to engage constructively with the process and to achieve a successful review. Given the size and capacity constraints of the Tongan Foreign Service and the prescriptive requirements of the UPR process, it was decided that the state would reach out to development partners and allies for assistance.

The assistance came, courtesy of the New Zealand Government, in the form of an adviser – a former judge with experience of the Pacific region. The co-ordination and preparation of the report involved an intense ten-day consultation period with 49 civil society organisations, including the chambers of commerce, the media, religious organisations, the private sector and other stakeholders. The Government was fully aware of NGO involvement in Tonga and was therefore committed to ensuring a wide consultative process.

The national consultative process was carried out as the capital was emerging from a difficult period following the riots of 2006. The consultation enabled a shift in focus from a disturbing past and paved the way for Tongans to openly exchange views in a calm and collective manner on the human rights record of their country. Such discussions were difficult at times, but the judge-adviser helped to entrench the necessary respect and demeanour.

The report was eventually accepted by all those involved in the process. Somewhat unusually, the consultation process resulted in consensus from all quarters. The national report was able not only to represent the views of the Government, but also to portray the views of civil society, NGOs and other stakeholders. Such consensus was deemed rather fortuitous and did not preclude the NGOs from submitting their own reports to the UPR process. The finalised report was submitted first to the Prime Minister and then to the Cabinet. Following their approval, it was transmitted to the Human Rights Council.

Both because of the unfamiliarity of the UPR process and the absence of a Tonga diplomatic mission in Geneva, many practical elements of the UPR were unclear. Concerns included how best to present the report to the HRC and how the three-hour interactive dialogue would turn out in reality. Despite these practical concerns, Tonga was committed to delivering the best possible results of the process.

*Contributed by Viliami Malolo, Deputy Permanent Representative, Permanent Mission to the United Nations in New York, previously with the Ministry of Foreign Affairs, Tonga.

Tongan officials observed the first UPR working group session in April 2008 in order to gain an overview of the process and to help decide on the composition of the Tongan delegation for their own working group session in May 2008. It was decided that a high-level delegation made up of the Foreign Minister, the UN Ambassador, the UK High Commissioner and a Foreign Service official would represent Tonga.

Tonga approached the UPR process with much enthusiasm. During the interactive dialogue 34 states made comments and asked questions. Most statements were definite recommendations and were proposed in a straightforward manner.

The Tongan delegation, through the Foreign Minister, accepted 31 recommendations and rejected 11. In June 2008, Tonga returned to the HRC for the final adoption of the report. There were no further changes or amendments. Tonga found value in this last one-hour session due to the opportunity to make residual comments and to listen to the NGOs who are given a platform to highlight issues that they feel are important.

In Tonga's experience, the NGOs made interesting comments and the state was receptive to this dialogue as a part of the process. The only concern was that many of the NGOs present at this session were international organisations. Tonga's opinion was that there should be more opportunity for local NGOs, who work in the country under review, to make representations to the HRC.

In terms of the follow-up, Tonga was made aware of the trust fund for financial assistance towards capacity building and technical assistance. When this fund is operational, Tonga is keen to make use of financial and technical assistance in the following specific areas of concern: greater training and opportunities for civil society organisations; civic and educational programmes focusing on reconciliation; assistance on treaty ratification; and assistance in ongoing constitutional and political reform.

Overall, Tonga's experience of the UPR was that the process presented a great opportunity to share with the world 'the Tongan story'. The process particularly emphasised dialogue, not only in Geneva, but by facilitating many opportunities for follow-up conversations and offers of assistance. In addition, Tonga believes that it succeeded in delivering its report to the best of standards because there was a political will within Tonga to fully embrace the UPR. Tonga is keen to build on the momentum of the UPR process and is considering sharing its report with intergovernmental organisations such as the European Commission. It is hoped that sharing Tonga's experience with others will enable human rights achievements on the ground as a result of further discussions and collaboration.

What National Human Rights Institutions Can Do to Get the Most from the UPR[*]

Introduction

As independent national bodies with constitutional or legislative mandates to pro-tect and promote human rights, Paris Principles[6] compliant NHRIs are able to effec-tively contribute to the UPR mechanism before, during and after the working group sessions in Geneva in the following ways:

1. Before the UPR

NHRIs can undertake the following strategies during the preliminary period:

• *Participate effectively in the government's UPR national consultations*

NHRIs should take a proactive approach to ensure that their input is taken into consideration and reflected in the national UPR report. NHRIs should therefore participate actively and effectively in any pre-UPR national consultations organ-ised by their governments.

• *Contribute to the OHCHR's summary of stakeholders' information*

In addition, NHRIs are strongly encouraged to prepare and submit an indepen-dent report to the Office of the High Commissioner for Human Rights. NHRIs should organise their own consultations with civil society and government in the preparation of their independent reports. The scope, structure, format and deadline of the report should strictly follow the OHCHR's technical guidelines.[7]

2. During the UPR

During the UPR, NHRIs can contribute to the UPR working group session in the following ways:

• *Observe the live interactive dialogue*

If NHRIs can send representatives to Geneva during the UPR working group session, they will be able to attend and observe the UPR interactive dialogue (but not make any direct interventions). NHRIs that cannot travel to Geneva

---

*Contributed by Kieren Fitzpatrick, Director of the Asia Pacific Forum of National Human Rights Institutions (APF)

should still be able to view the live webcast of their government's UPR session on the OHCHR website.[8]

- *Deliver a statement upon adoption of the UPR final report*

    Following the adoption of the final UPR report by the HRC, NHRIs in Geneva may request the opportunity to make a two-minute oral statement. NHRIs that cannot travel to Geneva may wish to seek the assistance of an accredited regional NHRI co-ordinating committee[9] or the resident representative of the International Coordinating Committee of NHRIs (ICC) to present the statement on their behalf.

3. After the UPR

It is after both the UPR working group session and the adoption of the final UPR report that NHRIs have the most potential to use the UPR to strengthen human rights in-country. The Asia Pacific Forum makes four suggestions:

- *Publicise and disseminate the outcomes of the UPR*

    NHRIs can publicise the outcomes of the UPR as this will provide added impetus to governments to implement their pledges and accepted recommendations. NHRIs may choose to do this through releasing a press statement or calling a press conference.

- *Synchronise internal work plans with the UPR*

    The recommendations and commitments within the final UPR report can be an important tool for informing the future direction of the NHRI's work. Where appropriate, NHRIs may wish to consider streamlining their forthcoming activities and internal work plan with the UPR outcomes.

- *Organise post-UPR consultations*

    NHRIs are encouraged to organise post-UPR consultations with government and with civil society with the aim of establishing a timeline and plan of action for the government's implementation of the UPR recommendations.

    NHRIs can also assist their governments develop plans for mainstreaming the UPR recommendations throughout national planning and legislative review processes.

- *Monitor the implementation of UPR outcomes*

    NHRIs can play an important role by acting as a 'watch-dog' to assess the extent to which their governments have implemented the pledges and recommendations made during the UPR mechanism. NHRIs may wish to consider using their annual reports as a tool for monitoring implementation. Their assessments should also be reflected in their next independent report to the OHCHR for the second cycle of their state's UPR.

Conclusion

The UPR is still a relatively new and evolving mechanism. It therefore remains to be seen to what extent it will be effective in improving the human rights situation at the national level. Nonetheless, what is certain is that NHRIs can and should play a role in the process, to enable the UPR to fulfil its true potential as a tool for positive change.

Group discussion during the UPR seminar for Commonwealth countries reporting in 2009, held in November 2008 at the Commonwealth Secretariat, London.

What Civil Society Organisations Can Do to Get the Most from the UPR*

Introduction

All relevant stakeholders, including civil society organisations, can and should contribute to the UPR in various ways and at all phases of the process.[10]

Civil society organisations should engage with the UPR because the process represents a unique opportunity to strengthen dialogue and co-operation between the state, NHRIs and CSOs, as well as among CSOs, concerning the implementation of human rights at national level.

The UPR provides for the participation of 'all relevant stakeholders'.[11] Currently, participation of CSOs from remote global areas, as well as CSOs representing marginalised groups, is low. However the UPR process is still new and unfamiliar to many, so this proportion can be expected to increase. In addition to CSOs, greater participation by the media, parliamentarians and academics can usefully support and complement the contribution of CSOs to the UPR.

During the preparation phase of the UPR

In the run-up to the actual review in Geneva, CSOs may engage in the UPR by submitting a report to the HRC and also by participating in the country's own national consultative process.

To prepare and collect information for submission to the UPR, CSOs can usefully organise regional and national information sessions and workshops to increase awareness of the UPR and to encourage and co-ordinate coalitions around priority issues. CSOs are also encouraged to seek consultation and co-ordination with the NHRI where one exists.

Regarding the content of a CSO's report, organisations are encouraged to remember that the UPR process upholds the principles of co-operation and non-confrontation. Best practice in this regard includes proposing constructive solutions (specific measures, policies, laws, etc.) for each of the challenges raised in the submission. CSOs are also encouraged to adhere strictly to the guidelines developed by the OHCHR.[12]

*Contributed by Cynthia Gervais, Director of the European Office of Rights and Democracy, Geneva.

Furthermore, CSOs can participate in the national consultations that will be conducted by the state under review when preparing their national report. CSOs can also open a dialogue with the SuR on the information they are preparing for their submission.

The UPR provides for the participation of 'all relevant stakeholders'.

During the review

CSOs can contribute further to the dissemination of relevant information to the representatives of countries who will participate in the interactive dialogue. Useful practices include suggesting questions and recommendations to be addressed to the SuR in line with the contents of the three reports that serve as the basis of the review.

CSOs can attend the interactive dialogue in Geneva. If this is not a viable option, CSOs can instead organise meetings with relevant stakeholders at national level to watch it live through the webcast and discuss immediate follow-up prior to the adoption of the outcome of the UPR.

CSOs can intervene in the plenary meeting of the HRC dedicated to the adoption of the outcome of the UPR. They can usefully co-ordinate among themselves, as well as with the NHRI where one exists, to make the best use of the 20 minutes allocated overall to their interventions.

During the follow-up

Emerging CSO practices with regard to the follow-up of the UPR include:

(a) Participation in the debate under the new item 6 on the agenda of the regular sessions of the HRC dedicated to the UPR;

(b) Participation in the establishment of a timetable and of systematic follow-up mechanisms for the outcome of the UPR at the national level.

The role of international non-governmental organisations

In addition to making their own contribution, international non-governmental organisations (INGOs) can provide support, particularly in developing countries, by sharing knowledge with and building the capacity of relevant stakeholders to enable them to participate meaningfully in the UPR.

Conclusion

By engaging in the UPR, CSOs can help identify and overcome challenges and promote best practices that impact on the credibility and effectiveness of the UPR mechanism.

Through their meaningful participation in the UPR, CSOs, together with states and NHRIs, can contribute to making the UPR a genuine opportunity for the achievement of measurable results in the improvement of the realisation of human rights on the ground.

Section III

THE FIRST YEAR OF THE UPR: ANALYSIS AND SUMMARY

UPR Year One

The UK, India and South Africa took part in the UPR at the Human Rights Council in April 2008. Ghana, Pakistan, Zambia, Sri Lanka and Tonga appeared in May 2008 and Botswana, The Bahamas, Barbados and Tuvalu appeared in December 2008, making a total of 12 Commonwealth states in the first year of the UPR. All but one of these countries attended a preparatory seminar on the UPR run by the Secretariat in March 2008.

Each country took its own approach to the preparation of its report (Annex 6), including the consultation element. Each composed its delegation on its own lines and is drawing up its implementation plans according to its own circumstances. A strong message that emerges from this work is that there is no single model for either consultation or preparation of the report. The approaches of Zambia and Tonga, for example, differ greatly, yet both are perfectly valid. This publication seeks to bring some of this information to the larger debate about the UPR and to assist states that are now preparing, or will soon be considering how they will prepare, for the UPR. It also shares the initial experiences of stakeholders and considers how they can maximise the UPR process.

Preparation and consultation: Zambia and Tonga

Zambia and Tonga face very different local conditions.

Tonga has a small population of just over 100,000 (2008) and is made up of over 170 small islands. It relies on tourism for much of its income and is making moves towards democracy. 2006 saw the eruption of political violence. The country has a small government infrastructure and felt the need to bring in external expertise for consultation and the production of its report.

The UPR preparation and process was seen by the government as a positive opportunity to build new processes nationally and focus attention on the future. The primary lens was not to see this as an additional burden that had somehow to be borne, but as a positive path to be followed for national benefit.

As Tonga's Deputy Permanent Representative at the UN, Viliami Malolo, acknowledges in section 2 of this report, the consultation process was not always easy: it was 'difficult at times', but made possible a valuable conversation about Tonga's human rights record. Respect was necessary, notes Mr Malolo, and was ensured, resulting in a report that enjoyed support from many stakeholders. He also appreciated hearing the input of stakeholders.

In contrast, Zambia is a large landlocked country with a population of more than 12 million. The Ministry of Justice took responsibility for the UPR report production process and undertook a major country-wide consultation that covered all nine provinces. These consultation sessions, each lasting three days, shared information about state obligations under international human rights law and the UPR process, as well as gathering material for the national report. Five ministries were involved in this process and a draft report was circulated to stakeholders. A final consultation, held in Lusaka, involved 31 government institutions, eight statutory and constitutional bodies, six media organisations and 43 CSOs.

The first year of the UPR saw an impressive wave of ratifications, signatures and removal of reservations across the Commonwealth

While the Tongan process is unlikely to be replicable in the Zambian context, the reverse is also true. Each was appropriate for the country and showed a commitment to the UPR process. Both countries produced reports that fully accepted the process, that were frank in their assessment of the local context and that were very well received in the Geneva review discussion.

The UPR as motivation for compliance: The Bahamas and Pakistan

The Geneva dialogue process enables states to share both achievements and challenges in the domestic human rights agenda; arising from these it is expected that there will be agreement on steps for further action. Many states are realising that significant steps can be taken either in the run-up to or at the Geneva element of the process: ratification of international treaties is among these possibilities. Some countries undertake ratifications before they appear at the HRC; some announce their intention to ratify during their presentation.

The first year of the UPR saw an impressive wave of ratifications, signatures and removal of reservations across the Commonwealth (see Annex 7). While it cannot be definitively concluded that a causal link exists between these events, it is reasonable to assume that there may indeed be a positive association.

There were 30 ratifications and signatures of international treaties and/or their protocols in 2008.[13] Sixteen of these were by states undergoing UPR in 2008 and 2009; that is over 50 per cent of all Commonwealth ratifications and signatures that took place in 2008. Three reservations to treaties were removed by Commonwealth countries in 2008, all against the Convention on the Rights of the Child (one by Mauritius and two by the UK).

Notable examples in terms of ratifications include The Bahamas, which promised to accept international standards during its UPR presentation and then ratified the International Covenant on Civil and Political Rights (ICCPR) and the International Covenant on Economic, Social and Cultural Rights (ICESCR), and afterwards signed the Convention Against Torture (CAT); and Pakistan, which ratified the ICESCR.

Themes raised – general and specific

This report includes a set of graphs that present information about the Geneva elements of the UPR as experienced by Commonwealth members. Drawing from the interactive dialogues, the graphs present the themes that were raised in comments, questions or recommendations for each of the 12 states. These are themes, not recommendations. The purpose of the HRU in undertaking this analysis is to show the nature of the interest shown in the first year of the UPR and this is indeed instructive. The UNHCHR outcome documents record the recommendations and their acceptance or otherwise by the states under review; the HRU does not duplicate these. Instead, the graphs analyse themes by country and by the most popular themes across Commonwealth countries.

As is to be expected, some themes raised are specific to the country under review. For example, the issue of an independent judiciary in Pakistan, child soldiers in Sri Lanka, judicial accountability in Ghana and a specific court case in Tuvalu were raised in discussion. The human rights dimensions of contemporary or historical events can rightly be raised in the interactive dialogue. By way of preparation, states may wish to consider and be prepared to respond to, or even proactively raise, contextual human rights concerns.

Emerging common themes

The first year of the UPR witnessed the emergence of a number of common areas of interest that were raised across countries. While analyses that have been undertaken by other agencies may show a broader picture, the HRU offers here an indication of the most popular themes raised in the interactive dialogues of Commonwealth states. Graph 13 highlights four dominant themes: gender equality and violence against women; child rights; human rights institutions; and ratification of international treaties. A year's data are not enough for firm conclusions to be reached, but they do reveal patterns that may become trends. These four areas suggest that there is an international consensus that:

- Supports and encourages gender equality;

- Opposes and seeks the end of violence against women;

- Strongly supports the rights of children, including the right to be free of physical punishment;

- Considers there is a need for national mechanisms that promote and protect human rights, especially NHRIs;

- States must sign up to and implement human rights standards, as set out in human rights treaties.

Furthermore, although they were not numerically dominant, other themes were raised for most Commonwealth states. They included the need for human rights training for various uniformed and legal professionals; prison conditions and the treatment of prisoners; HIV/AIDs and human rights; same-sex relationships; the death penalty (in countries which have not already abolished it); poverty and economic rights; and engagement with UN special procedures.

Once again, being aware of these areas of interest can help states in their preparation for the interactive dialogue.

Delegations

Several states under review sent high-level delegations to Geneva for the UPR mechanism (Annex 8). These often included ministers, as well as senior officials, and on occasion delegations were quite large. Both small states and others have taken this approach, signalling the seriousness with which they take the UPR and suggesting goodwill and intent for the promotion of human rights in their national contexts. Such profiles have been noted and appreciated in Geneva.

Another impact of high-level delegations is that they can encourage high-level engagement in the interactive dialogue from diplomatic missions in Geneva. If this does become the norm, it will give the UPR a profile that can offer further potential towards buy-in at government level for the promotion of human rights on the ground – that is, the *process* discussed in this report, as well as the *mechanism*.

The meaning of universality

The word 'universal' in the Universal Periodic Review, is intended to indicate that all states are subject to the review process. Implicit in this is the principle of equal treatment for all states – all have to go through the same mechanism and are treated in the same way procedurally.

Yet the word universal has a long history in human rights discourse and struggles. The Universal Declaration of Human Rights maps out a wide range of rights, drawing together areas subsequently separated and fought over: civil and political rights on the one hand, and economic, social and cultural rights on the other. It speaks to all humans – not only to women, children or the disabled, or any other specific group of people. Treaties that speak to specific groups – of people and rights – have an important role and should continue to enjoy full recognition and monitoring.

The UPR complements these and does so in a way that allows the situation or needs of specific groups to be brought to the fore, and allows either 'group' of rights to receive attention. Countries that have felt or argued the relative neglect of economic, social and cultural rights in international discourse can pay attention to these in their reviews. To do this at the expense of other rights would be problematic, but to draw all rights together into one conversation is a valuable exercise. The UPR can thereby complement treaty body mechanisms and special procedures and should not replace them.

Commonwealth participation

This report draws on the experiences of Commonwealth members undergoing the UPR in 2008 (Annex 9). Discussion has so far centred on the states under review. Yet the participation of member states in the dialogues is also worth consideration. The graphs that follow show not only the themes raised in the interactive dialogues, but also whether they were raised by Commonwealth members or by others.

In 2008, 12 members[14] of the HRC were Commonwealth states, though all states can participate in the interactive dialogue. During the 12 interactive dialogues involving Commonwealth member states, the 12 missions raised a range of issues – from violence against women and children to the death penalty, the need for ratification of human rights conventions, prison concerns, vulnerable groups, climate change, homosexuality and NHRIs. It is clear that there is an interest in the the whole range of human rights issues across the Commonwealth.

The 12 Commonwealth states reviewed in 2008 received 291 recommendations from states, including 18 to South Africa; 21 to Tonga; 35 to Sri Lanka; and 23 to Barbados. While the range of issues raised by Commonwealth states was wide (Table 1), the numerical profile of the states making recommendations was limited. Of the 291 recommendations, 62 (one-fifth) came from the Commonwealth.

One factor that features in this profile is that many small states do not have representation in Geneva. Only one-third of the Caribbean states and none of the Pacific island states maintain offices there. The appearance of the first Pacific small island state, Tonga, was met with much appreciation and a warm welcome. Commonwealth engagement in the UPR would be strengthened by a wider representation for these states in Geneva. Initiatives are under discussion to address this gap.

Table 1

State under review	Recommendations by Commonwealth states	Recommendations by non-Commonwealth states
UK	4	12
India	5	13
South Africa	2	16
Ghana	2	16
Pakistan	6	33
Zambia	4	15
Sri Lanka	3	32
Tonga	4	17
Botswana	10	25
The Bahamas	9	18
Barbados	7	16
Tuvalu	6	16
Total	**62**	**229**

It has not been possible to provide an analysis of the recommendations accepted – which and how many – by each country. States under review have adopted various models in accepting, rejecting or otherwise dealing with recommendations (Annex 10). This has proved to be a difficult dataset to compile for a number of reasons: some states have accepted some, but not all, of one or several recommendations (if a recommendation is complex, a state may agree with part but not all of it); some have decided that consultations with colleagues in the capital are required and we do not know the outcome of those discussions. There will need to be a systematic recording of these in order to make for a sensible and informed discussion in the second round of appearances in Geneva in four years time.

It is hoped that over time Commonwealth states will become increasingly committed to the UPR process and that they will become a stronger collective voice. This will demonstrate in a clear way that the Commonwealth is promoting one of its fundamental organising principles – respect for human rights.

Follow-up

The UPR process is about the enabling of co-operative efforts in the promotion of human rights on a domestic stage. It is in the post-Geneva phase that the many or few recommendations accepted by the SuR need to be implemented.

One method through which implementation can be addressed is the adoption of a national action plan on human rights. Here, consultations and strategic planning can together shape timely follow-up. Such a plan can also help identify which ministries or other agencies take the lead on a recommendation, what resources and expertise are available in-country and what is needed from partners. A time-line can also be established with a group to monitor and review implementation.

The Commonwealth publication, *Commonwealth Model National Plan of Action on Human Rights*, is a useful follow-up tool. It is available from the Commonwealth Secretariat.

The human rights team at the Secretariat is also available to assist with implementation in specific ways. Areas of work include: human rights training for police officers, government officers, judges and magistrates; advice and support in the establishment of NHRIs; and advice on ratification of international human rights treaties. The team is ready to discuss these and other relevant inputs with member states.

Conclusion

The UPR is not a panacea for addressing all human rights issues; nor is it a perfect mechanism in itself. It is a novel approach to the promotion of human rights, one which is based on important principles – co-operation, universality, equality – and has garnered considerable goodwill.

The UPR has to face and deal with some difficulties. For example, the number of states wishing to be involved in the three-hour dialogue extends beyond the time available; the SuR is able to ignore recommendations if it wishes to, even though they may address accepted international norms or standards; and the entry of stakeholders in the Geneva agenda comes at a very late stage. Some interventions have been of such a nature that it is not clear if they just make comments, or if they also make recommendations. Sometimes they are both: sometimes neither. On the other hand, the number of recommendations put to states has in some cases been considerable and questions have been raised as to the practicability of such a massive task list, if it is not matched by a commensurate commitment of resources and expertise – and political will.

The Secretariat notes that the potential of the UPR is considerable and the first year of operation has shown much promise. States have shown admirable commitment to the process and have welcomed the new approach that is transparent[15] and supports co-operation across countries. One year into the Geneva reviews many are positively impressed not only by the effort and goodwill brought to the debate, but also that there are increasingly substantive discussions of human rights, and not the political or ideological game-playing that some had feared.

Analysis of Topics Raised

The graphs that follow show what topics were raised in the three-hour interactive dialogue for each Commonwealth state that appeared in Geneva for the UPR. They are presented here in the chronological order in which the countries appeared in Geneva for the UPR session. They show how many times each topic was raised in a comment or question by Commonwealth and non-Commonwealth states. One comment may raise several issues and thus the totals in the graphs may be more than the questions or comments put to each state.

Graph 1. United Kingdom

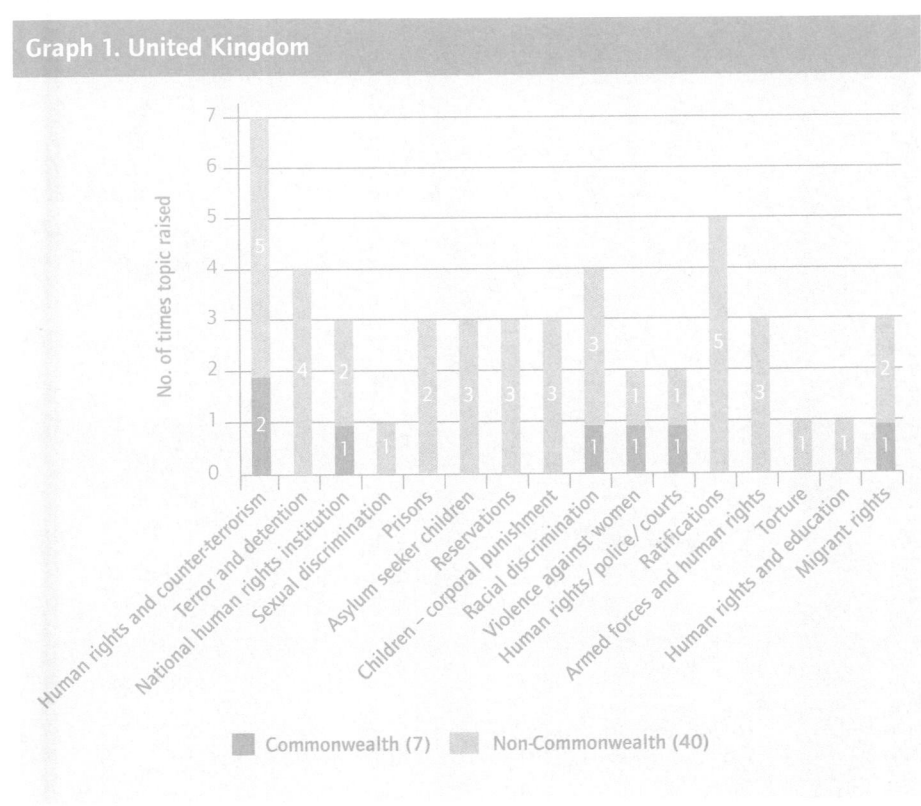

Graph 2. India

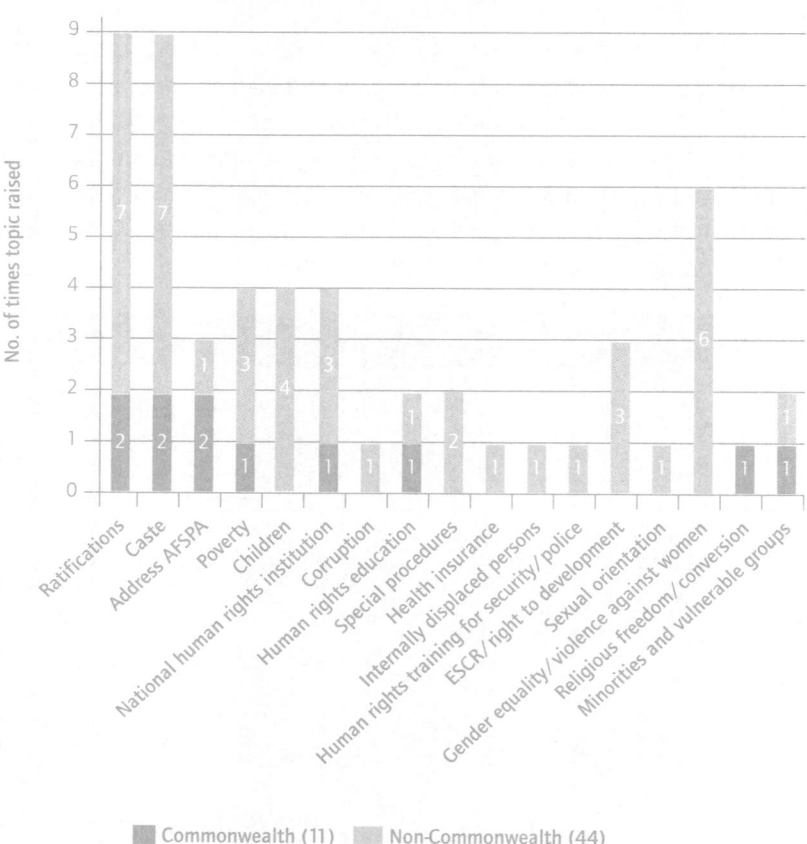

Commonwealth (11)   Non-Commonwealth (44)

Graph 3. South Africa

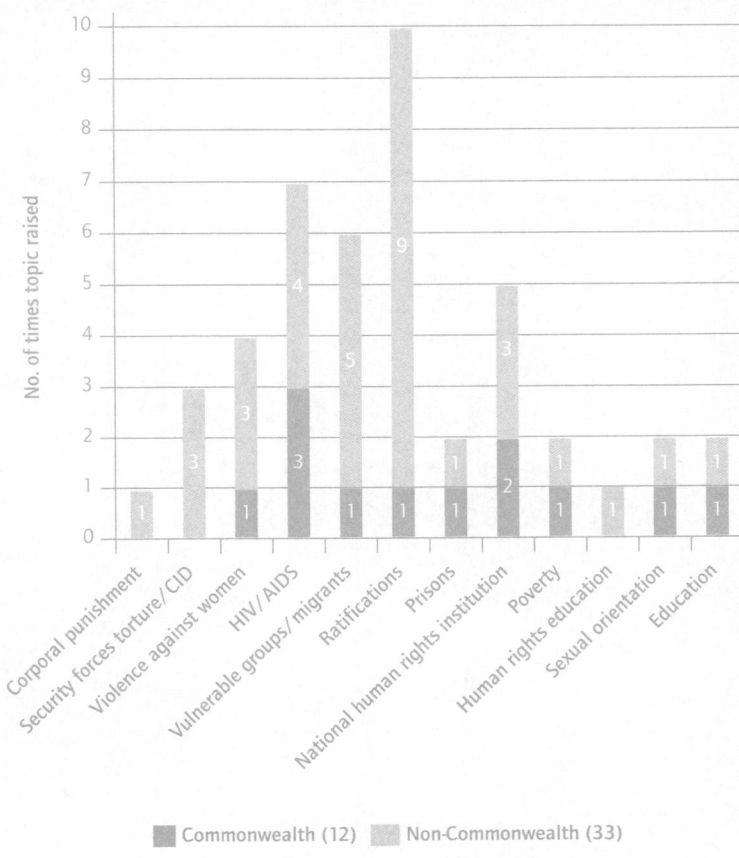

No. of times topic raised

Corporal punishment
Security forces torture/CID
Violence against women
HIV/AIDS
Vulnerable groups/migrants
Ratifications
Prisons
National human rights institution
Poverty
Human rights education
Sexual orientation
Education

■ Commonwealth (12) ■ Non-Commonwealth (33)

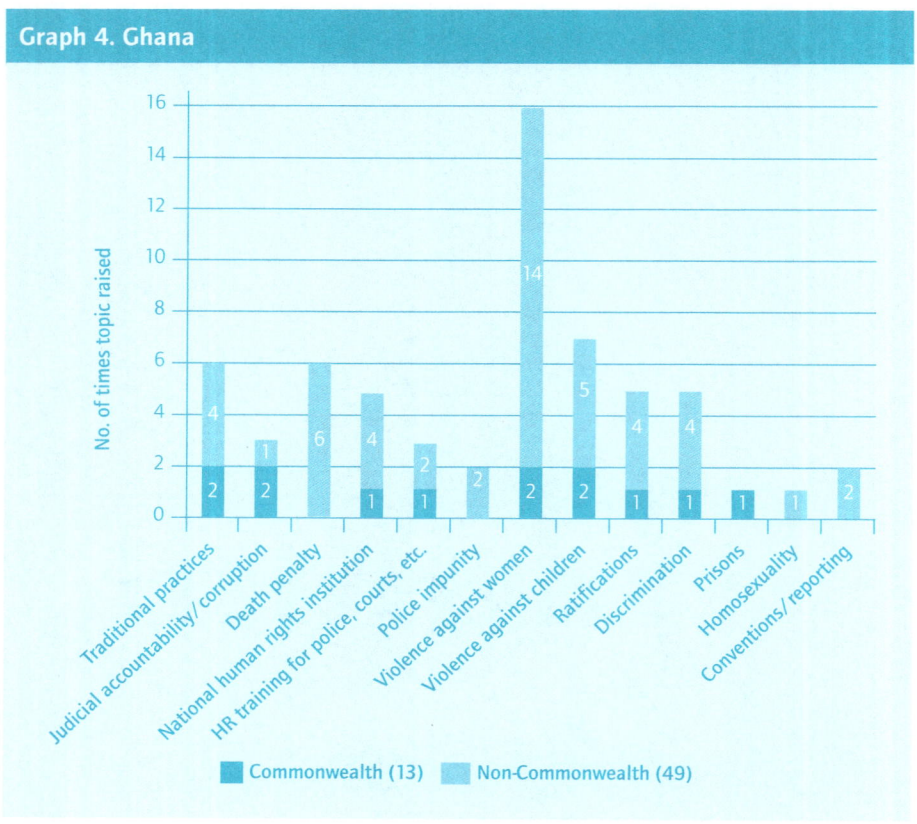

Graph 4. Ghana

No. of times topic raised

Commonwealth (13)   Non-Commonwealth (49)

Traditional practices
Judicial accountability/ corruption
Death penalty
National human rights institution
HR training for police, courts, etc.
Police impunity
Violence against women
Violence against children
Ratifications
Discrimination
Prisons
Homosexuality
Conventions/ reporting

Graph 5. Pakistan

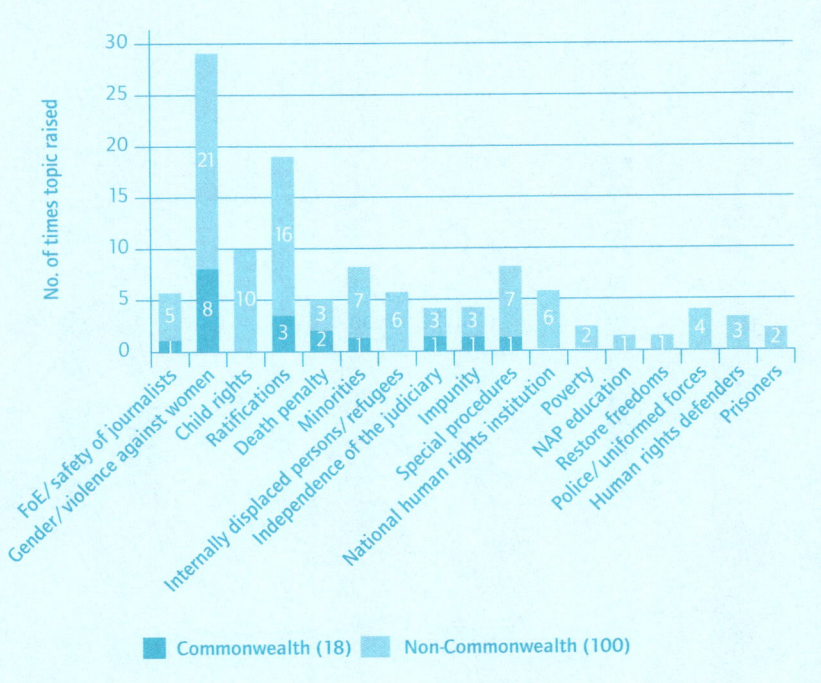

Graph 6. Zambia

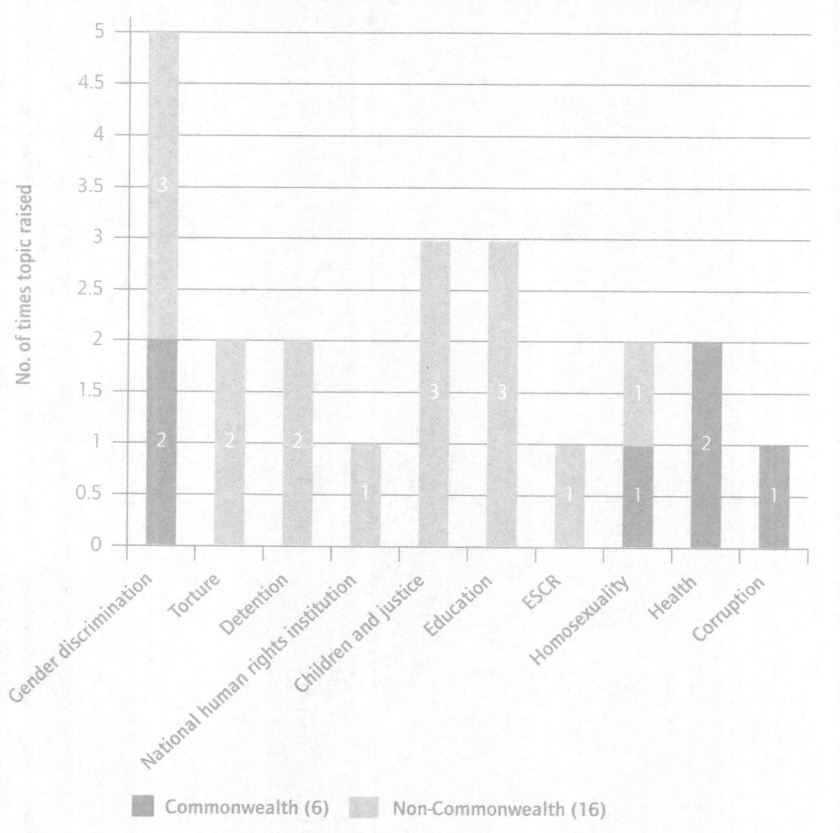

Graph 7. Sri Lanka

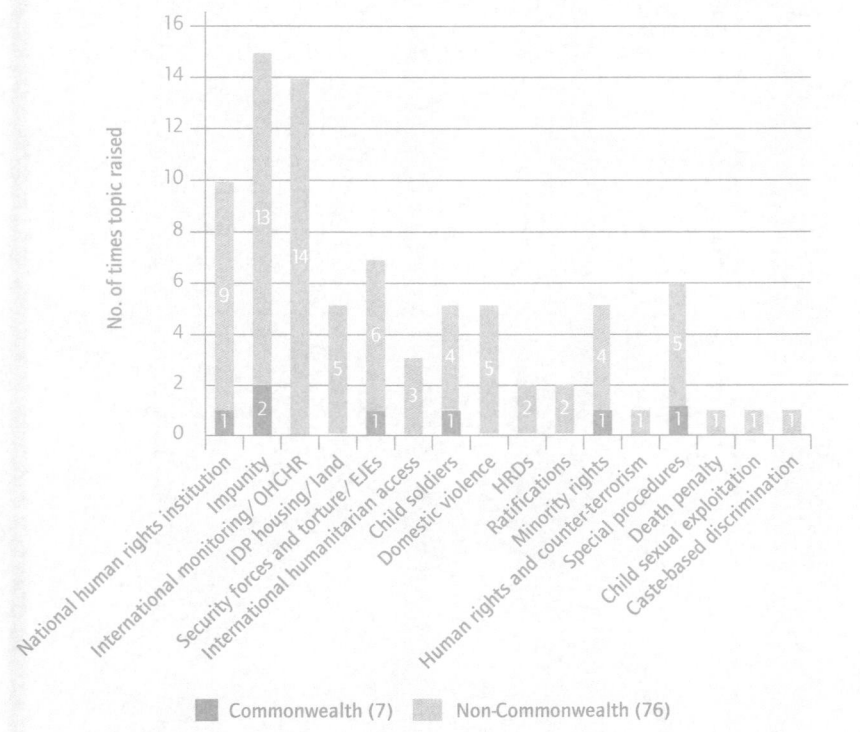

No. of times topic raised

Commonwealth (7)   Non-Commonwealth (76)

Graph 8. Tonga

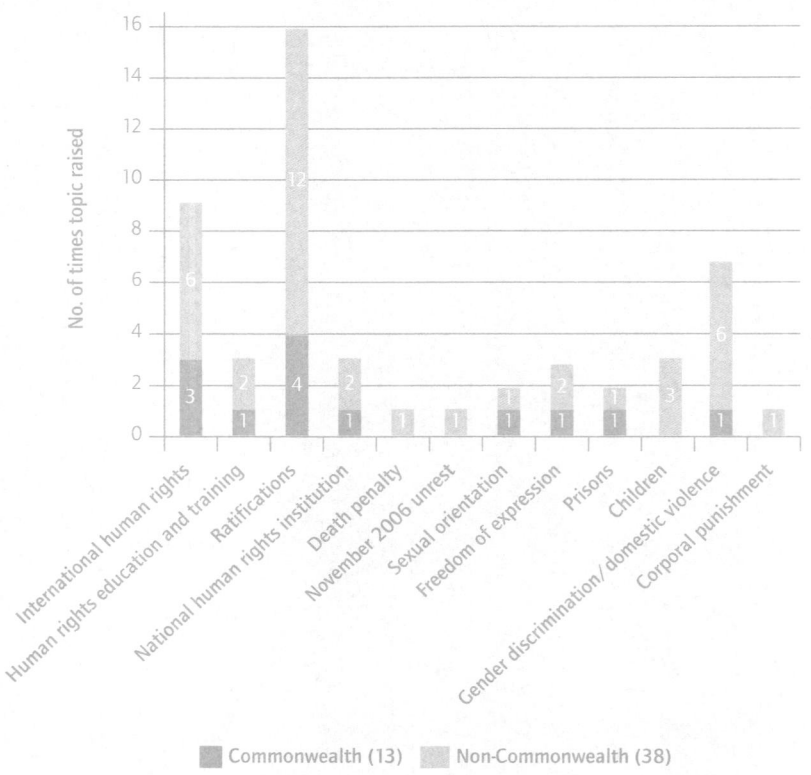

No. of times topic raised

International human rights
Human rights education and training
Ratifications
National human rights institution
Death penalty
November 2006 unrest
Sexual orientation
Freedom of expression
Prisons
Children
Gender discrimination/ domestic violence
Corporal punishment

■ Commonwealth (13)   ▨ Non-Commonwealth (38)

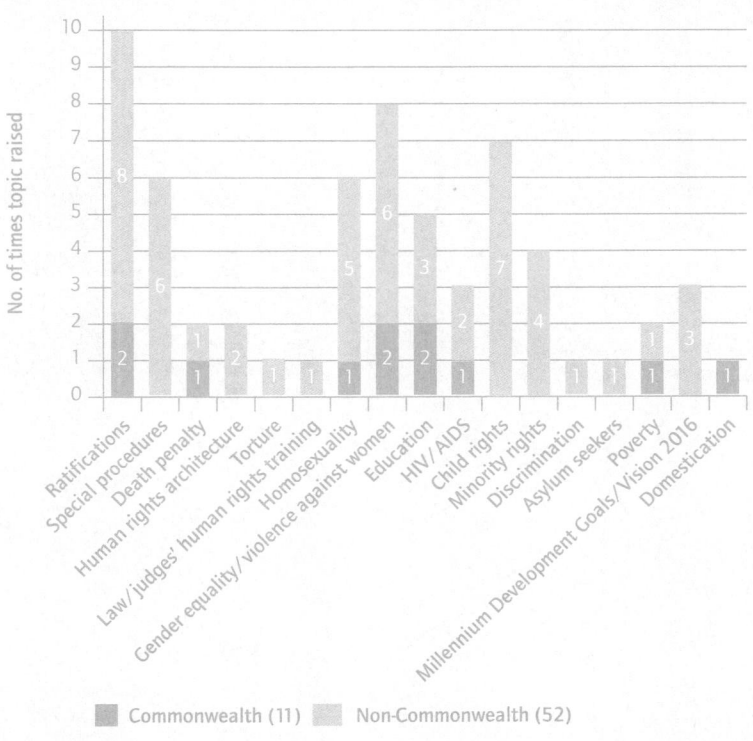

Graph 9. Botswana

Commonwealth (11)   Non-Commonwealth (52)

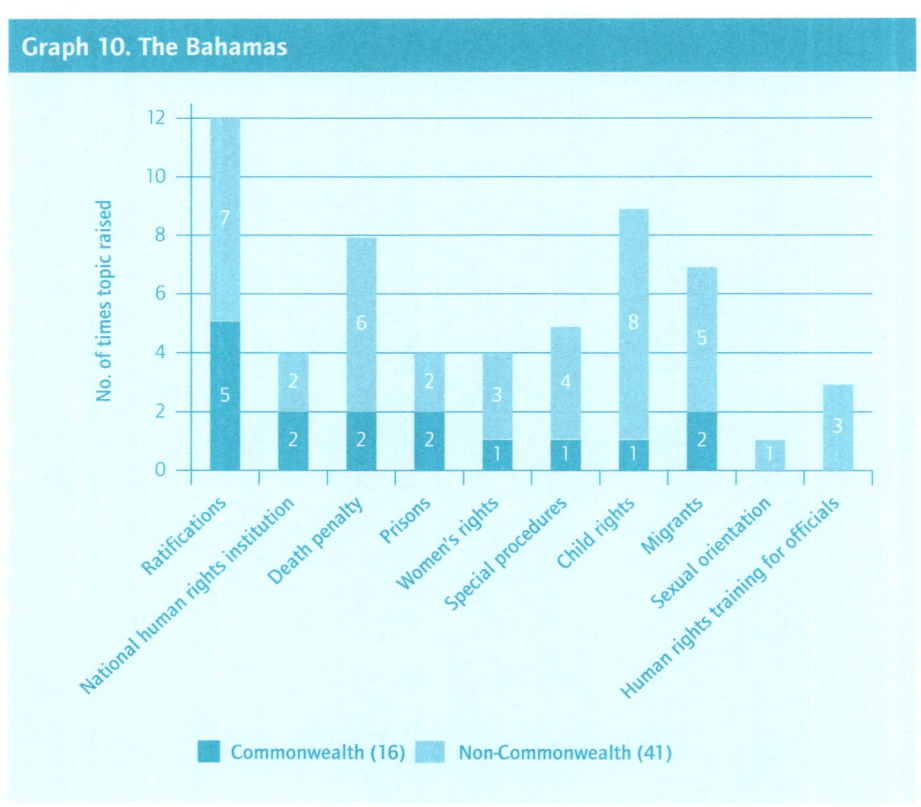

Graph 10. The Bahamas

No. of times topic raised

Ratifications: 5, 7
National human rights institution: 2, 2
Death penalty: 2, 6
Prisons: 2, 2
Women's rights: 1, 3
Special procedures: 1, 4
Child rights: 1, 8
Migrants: 2, 5
Sexual orientation: 1
Human rights training for officials: 3

■ Commonwealth (16)   ■ Non-Commonwealth (41)

Graph 11. Barbados

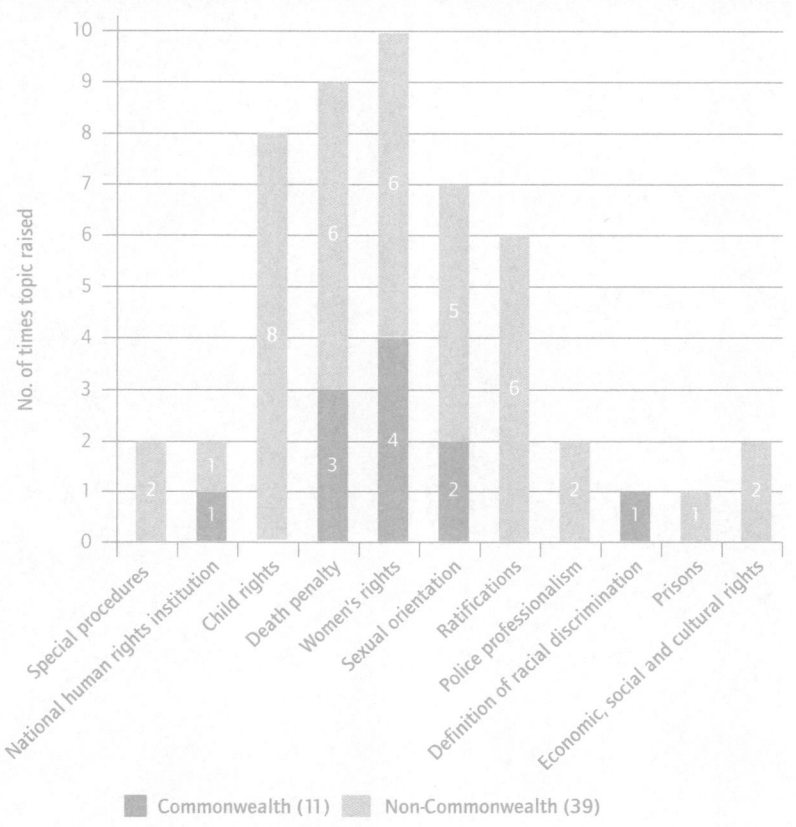

Commonwealth (11) ■ Non-Commonwealth (39)

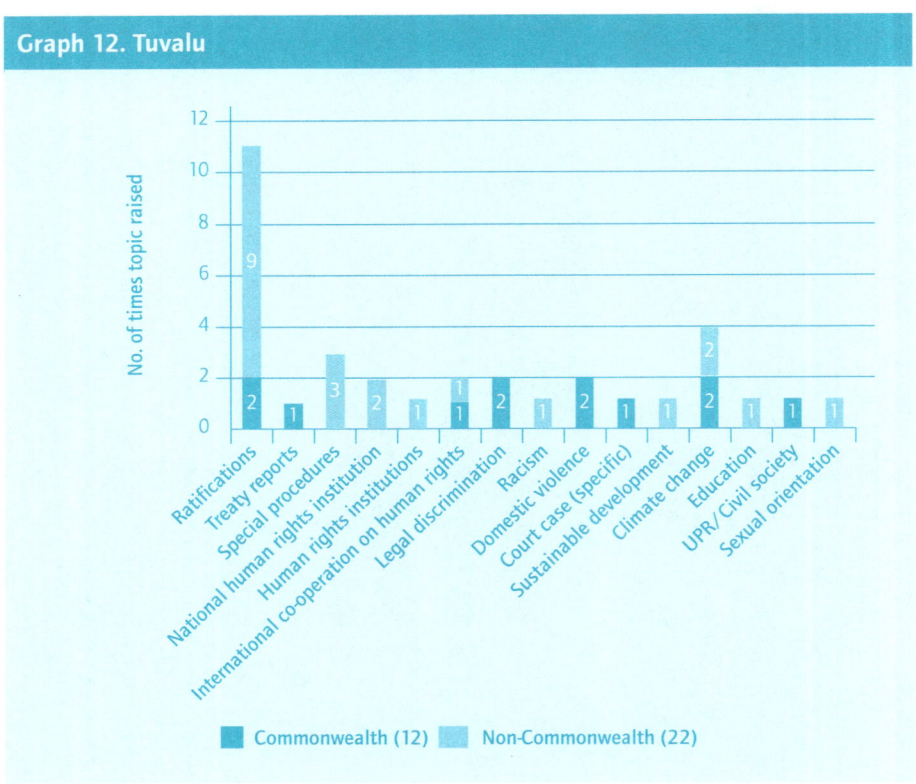

Graph 12. Tuvalu

No. of times topic raised

Commonwealth (12)　Non-Commonwealth (22)

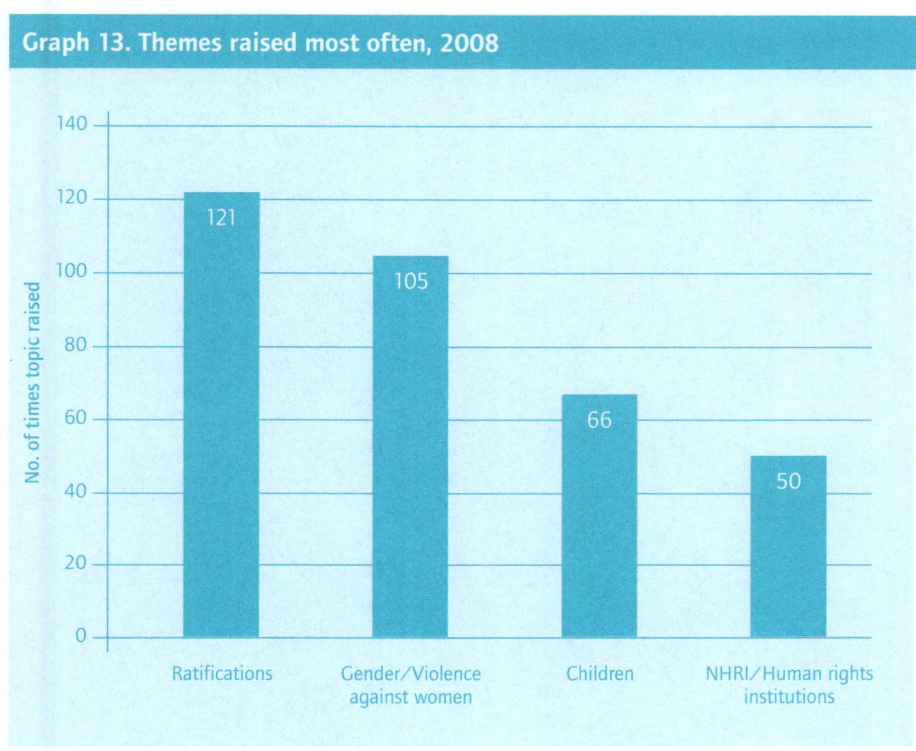

Graph 13. Themes raised most often, 2008

No. of times topic raised

Ratifications: 121	Gender/Violence against women: 105	Children: 66	NHRI/Human rights institutions: 50

UPR seminar for countries reporting in 2009, Commonwealth Secretariat, London, November 2008.

Summary of Recommendations

This section presents a collection of best practices and suggestions compiled from contributors' articles, as well as from the Secretariat's Human Rights Unit's work during the first year of the UPR.

For states

General approach to the UPR

- States should undertake a genuine assessment of their human rights situation, discuss challenges with peers during the UPR and be willing to initiate steps to improve the human rights situation in-country.

- Approaching the UPR process with positive political will can help facilitate opportunities for follow-up discussion and encourage offers of assistance.

- Given the commonalities in institutional and administrative systems, Commonwealth governments could work together to streamline internal processes governing the UPR and also evolve Commonwealth best practices.

Towards preparing for the review in Geneva

- Consultation with stakeholders (NHRIs and CSOs) in the preparation of the national report, as stipulated in Resolution 5/1, is a key component of success.

- It is important to disseminate information to the NHRI (where one exists) and CSOs in order to ensure their better understanding of the UPR process.

- Follow and publish a timeline for a transparent and inclusive consultative process. It would be helpful to hold consultations before the stakeholder's own UPR submission deadline.

- Forego a narrative style of reporting; instead evaluate achievements and challenges.

- If applicable, make contact with the diplomatic mission based in Geneva. The mission may be able to provide information regarding useful trends at the HRC.

- For states that have no office in Geneva, it would prove useful to work and communicate with other missions to gather such information.

- Keep an updated directory containing contact details of government officials and departments in charge of UPR processes and elements.

- Developing states could consider the need for financial help from the voluntary trust fund to facilitate participation in the UPR.

After Geneva

- Disseminate widely to the public information about the UPR experience and the recommendations accepted.

- Continue the consultative process with stakeholders when implementing the accepted recommendations.

- Developing states could make enquiries regarding the voluntary fund for financial and technical assistance for help with implementing recommendations. Third party countries/organisations may be willing to offer similar assistance. The HRU is available to offer expertise.

For stakeholders (NHRIs and CSOs)

Towards preparing for the review in Geneva

- Participate in any pre-UPR consultations held by the government to ensure relevant input is given.

- As the UPR process upholds the principles of co-operation and non-confrontation, stakeholder reports could focus on proposing constructive solutions to each challenge raised.

- Observe the UPR working session, either in Geneva or on the webcast.

- For CSOs:
  - Consider whether to submit one stakeholder report representing the views of a single organisation or whether to submit a joint consolidated report with other CSOs.

  - Partake in advocacy by suggesting questions and recommendations to other states for them to address to the state under review during the interactive dialogue.

After Geneva

- Increase public awareness and publish the recommendations and commitments accepted by the government, for example in an annual report or press release.

- Encourage the government's adherence to recommendations accepted and assess the extent to which the government has implemented its pledges.

This can be done through organising post-UPR consultations with government to establish a timeline and plan of action for implementation.

- Align work plan and activities with the outcomes of the UPR.

Notes

1   See Annex 1.
2   See Annex 2.
3   Commonwealth Human Rights Initiative – for further information on its experiences as a NGO in the UPR process, see p. 18.
4   Commonwealth Secretariat, Commonwealth Model National Plan of Action on Human Rights (London, 2007).
5   For example, Nico Schrijver, 'UN Human Rights Council: A New "Society of the Committed" or Just Old Wine in New Bottles?', *Leiden Journal of International Law*, 20 (2007), pp. 809–23; Balakrishnan Rajagopal, 'Lipstick on a Caterpillar? Assessing the New UN Human Rights Council through Historical Reflection', *Buffalo Human Rights Law Review*, 13; Helen Upton, 'The Human Rights Council: First Impression and Future Challenges', *Human Rights Law Review*, 7(1), pp. 29–39; Claire Callejon, 'Developments at the Human Rights Council in 2007: A Reflection of its Ambivalence', *Human Rights Law Review*, 8(2), pp. 323–42.
6   Principles relating to the status and functioning of National Institutions for the Protection and Promotion of Human Rights ('the Paris Principles'), UN General Assembly Resolution A/RES/48/134 of 20 December 1993.
7   Available at the OHCHR's website at: http://www.ohchr.org/EN/HRBodies/UPR/Documents/TechnicalGuideEN.pdf
8   The homepage for the HRC webcast site can be found at: www.un.org/webcast/unhrc/index.asp. The site will show live webcasts during each UPR Working Session. Following the sessions, each country's UPR webcast is archived on the website.
9   The Regional NHRI Coordinating Committees which can be accredited to speak before the HRC are: African Network of National Human Rights Institutions, Asia Pacific Forum of National Human Rights Institutions, European Coordinating Committee of National Human Rights Institutions and Inter-American Federation of National Human Rights Institutions.
10 For more information, please consult the website of the Office of the High Commissioner for Human Rights at http://www.ohchr.org/EN/HRBodies/UPR/Pages/NgosNhris.aspx
11 See Annex 1.
12 See Annex 5.
13 There were ten ratifications in the Commonwealth in 2007.
14 Bangladesh, Cameroon, Canada, Ghana, India, Malaysia, Mauritius, Nigeria, Pakistan, South Africa, UK and Zambia.
15 All UPR documents are made available on the OHCHR website, http://www.ohchr.org/EN/HRBodies/UPR/Pages/Documentation.aspx

Human Rights Council Resolution 5/1*

5/1. Institution-building of the United Nations Human Rights Council

The Human Rights Council,

Acting in compliance with the mandate entrusted to it by the United Nations General Assembly in resolution 60/251 of 15 March 2006,

Having considered the draft text on institution-building submitted by the President of the Council,

1. *Adopts* the draft text entitled 'United Nations Human Rights Council: Institution Building', as contained in the annex to the present resolution, including its appendix(ces);

2. *Decides* to submit the following draft resolution to the General Assembly for its adoption as a matter of priority in order to facilitate the timely implementation of the text contained thereafter:

'*The General Assembly,*

'*Taking note* of Human Rights Council resolution 5/1 of 18 June 2007,

'1. *Welcomes* the text entitled 'United Nations Human Rights Council: Institution Building', as contained in the annex to the present resolution, including its appendix(ces).'

9th meeting
18 June 2007

[Resolution adopted without a vote.][1]

---

[1]See A/HRC/5/21, chapter III, paras. 60–62.

*UN document. Please see: http://ap.ohchr.org/documents/E/HRC/resolutions/A_HRC_RES_5_1.doc

UNITED NATIONS HUMAN RIGHTS COUNCIL: INSTITUTION-BUILDING

I. UNIVERSAL PERIODIC REVIEW MECHANISM

A. Basis of the review

1. The basis of the review is:

   (a) The Charter of the United Nations;

   (b) The Universal Declaration of Human Rights;

   (c) Human rights instruments to which a State is party;

   (d) Voluntary pledges and commitments made by States, including those undertaken when presenting their candidatures for election to the Human Rights Council (hereinafter 'the Council').

2. In addition to the above and given the complementary and mutually interrelated nature of international human rights law and international humanitarian law, the review shall take into account applicable international humanitarian law.

B. Principles and objectives

1. Principles

3. The universal periodic review should:

   (*a*) Promote the universality, interdependence, indivisibility and interrelatedness of all human rights;

   (*b*) Be a cooperative mechanism based on objective and reliable information and on interactive dialogue;

   (*c*) Ensure universal coverage and equal treatment of all States;

   (*d*) Be an intergovernmental process, United Nations Member-driven and action-oriented;

   (*e*) Fully involve the country under review;

   (*f*) Complement and not duplicate other human rights mechanisms, thus representing an added value;

   (*g*) Be conducted in an objective, transparent, non-confrontational and non-politicized manner;

   (*h*) Not be overly burdensome to the concerned State or to the agenda of the Council;

   (*i*) Not be overly long; it should be realistic and not absorb a disproportionate amount of time, human and financial resources;

   (*j*) Not diminish the Council's capacity to respond to urgent human rights situations;

   (*k*) Fully integrate a gender perspective;

(*l*) Without prejudice to the obligations contained in the elements provided for in the basis of review, take into account the level of development and specificities of countries;

(*m*) Ensure the participation of all relevant stakeholders, including non-governmental organizations and national human rights institutions, in accordance with General Assembly resolution 60/251 of 15 March 2006 and Economic and Social Council resolution 1996/31 of 25 July 1996, as well as any decisions that the Council may take in this regard.

2. Objectives

4. The objectives of the review are:

(*a*) The improvement of the human rights situation on the ground;

(*b*) The fulfilment of the State's human rights obligations and commitments and assessment of positive developments and challenges faced by the State;

(*c*) The enhancement of the State's capacity and of technical assistance, in consultation with, and with the consent of, the State concerned;

(*d*) The sharing of best practice among States and other stakeholders;

(*e*) Support for cooperation in the promotion and protection of human rights;

(*f*) The encouragement of full cooperation and engagement with the Council, other human rights bodies and the Office of the United Nations High Commissioner for Human Rights.

C. Periodicity and order of the review

5. The review begins after the adoption of the universal periodic review mechanism by the Council.

6. The order of review should reflect the principles of universality and equal treatment.

7. The order of the review should be established as soon as possible in order to allow States to prepare adequately.

8. All member States of the Council shall be reviewed during their term of membership.

9. The initial members of the Council, especially those elected for one or two-year terms, should be reviewed first.

10. A mix of member and observer States of the Council should be reviewed.

11. Equitable geographic distribution should be respected in the selection of countries for review.

12. The first member and observer States to be reviewed will be chosen by the drawing of lots from each Regional Group in such a way as to ensure full respect for equitable

geographic distribution. Alphabetical order will then be applied beginning with those countries thus selected, unless other countries volunteer to be reviewed.

13. The period between review cycles should be reasonable so as to take into account the capacity of States to prepare for, and the capacity of other stakeholders to respond to, the requests arising from the review.

14. The periodicity of the review for the first cycle will be of four years. This will imply the consideration of 48 States per year during three sessions of the working group of two weeks each.[a]

D. Process and modalities of the review

1. Documentation

15. The documents on which the review would be based are:

   (a) Information prepared by the State concerned, which can take the form of a national report, on the basis of general guidelines to be adopted by the Council at its sixth session (first session of the second cycle), and any other information considered relevant by the State concerned, which could be presented either orally or in writing, provided that the written presentation summarizing the information will not exceed 20 pages, to guarantee equal treatment to all States and not to overburden the mechanism. States are encouraged to prepare the information through a broad consultation process at the national level with all relevant stake-holders;

   (b) Additionally a compilation prepared by the Office of the High Commissioner for Human Rights of the information contained in the reports of treaty bodies, special procedures, including observations and comments by the State concerned, and other relevant official United Nations documents, which shall not exceed 10 pages;

   (c) Additional, credible and reliable information provided by other relevant stakehold-ers to the universal periodic review which should also be taken into consideration by the Council in the review. The Office of the High Commissioner for Human Rights will prepare a summary of such information which shall not exceed 10 pages.

16. The documents prepared by the Office of the High Commissioner for Human Rights should be elaborated following the structure of the general guidelines adopted by the Council regarding the information prepared by the State concerned.

17. Both the State's written presentation and the summaries prepared by the Office of the High Commissioner for Human Rights shall be ready six weeks prior to the review by the working group to ensure the distribution of documents simultaneously in the six official languages of the United Nations, in accordance with General Assembly resolution 53/208 of 14 January 1999.

2. Modalities

18. The modalities of the review shall be as follows:

   (a) The review will be conducted in one working group, chaired by the President of the Council and composed of the 47 member States of the Council. Each member State will decide on the composition of its delegation;[b]

(b) Observer States may participate in the review, including in the interactive dialogue;

(c) Other relevant stakeholders may attend the review in the Working Group;

(d) A group of three rapporteurs, selected by the drawing of lots among the members of the Council and from different Regional Groups (troika) will be formed to facilitate each review, including the preparation of the report of the working group. The Office of the High Commissioner for Human Rights will provide the necessary assistance and expertise to the rapporteurs.

19. The country concerned may request that one of the rapporteurs be from its own Regional Group and may also request the substitution of a rapporteur on only one occasion.

20. A rapporteur may request to be excused from participation in a specific review process.

21. Interactive dialogue between the country under review and the Council will take place in the working group. The rapporteurs may collate issues or questions to be transmitted to the State under review to facilitate its preparation and focus the interactive dialogue, while guaranteeing fairness and transparency.

22. The duration of the review will be three hours for each country in the working group. Additional time of up to one hour will be allocated for the consideration of the outcome by the plenary of the Council.

23. Half an hour will be allocated for the adoption of the report of each country under review in the working group.

24. A reasonable time frame should be allocated between the review and the adoption of the report of each State in the working group.

25. The final outcome will be adopted by the plenary of the Council.

E. Outcome of the review

1. Format of the outcome

26. The format of the outcome of the review will be a report consisting of a summary of the proceedings of the review process; conclusions and/or recommendations, and the voluntary commitments of the State concerned.

2. Content of the outcome

27. The universal periodic review is a cooperative mechanism. Its outcome may include, inter alia:

(a) An assessment undertaken in an objective and transparent manner of the human rights situation in the country under review, including positive developments and the challenges faced by the country;

(*b*) Sharing of best practices;

(*c*) An emphasis on enhancing cooperation for the promotion and protection of human rights;

(*d*) The provision of technical assistance and capacity-building in consultation with, and with the consent of, the country concerned;[c]

(*e*) Voluntary commitments and pledges made by the country under review.

3. Adoption of the outcome

28. The country under review should be fully involved in the outcome.

29. Before the adoption of the outcome by the plenary of the Council, the State concerned should be offered the opportunity to present replies to questions or issues that were not sufficiently addressed during the interactive dialogue.

30. The State concerned and the member States of the Council, as well as observer States, will be given the opportunity to express their views on the outcome of the review before the plenary takes action on it.

31. Other relevant stakeholders will have the opportunity to make general comments before the adoption of the outcome by the plenary.

32. Recommendations that enjoy the support of the State concerned will be identified as such. Other recommendations, together with the comments of the State concerned thereon, will be noted. Both will be included in the outcome report to be adopted by the Council.

F. Follow-up to the review

33. The outcome of the universal periodic review, as a cooperative mechanism, should be implemented primarily by the State concerned and, as appropriate, by other relevant stakeholders.

34. The subsequent review should focus, inter alia, on the implementation of the preceding outcome.

35. The Council should have a standing item on its agenda devoted to the universal periodic review.

36. The international community will assist in implementing the recommendations and conclusions regarding capacity-building and technical assistance, in consultation with, and with the consent of, the country concerned.

37. In considering the outcome of the universal periodic review, the Council will decide if and when any specific follow-up is necessary.

38. After exhausting all efforts to encourage a State to cooperate with the universal periodic review mechanism, the Council will address, as appropriate, cases of persistent non-cooperation with the mechanism.

II. SPECIAL PROCEDURES

A. Selection and appointment of mandate-holders

39. The following general criteria will be of paramount importance while nominating, selecting and appointing mandate-holders: (a) expertise; (b) experience in the field of the mandate; (c) independence; (d) impartiality; (e) personal integrity; and (f) objectivity.

40. Due consideration should be given to gender balance and equitable geographic representation, as well as to an appropriate representation of different legal systems.

41. Technical and objective requirements for eligible candidates for mandate-holders will be approved by the Council at its sixth session (first session of the second cycle), in order to ensure that eligible candidates are highly qualified individuals who possess established competence, relevant expertise and extensive professional experience in the field of human rights.

42. The following entities may nominate candidates as special procedures mandate-holders: (a) Governments; (b) Regional Groups operating within the United Nations human rights system; (c) international organizations or their offices (e.g. the Office of the High Commissioner for Human Rights); (d) non-governmental organizations; (e) other human rights bodies; (f) individual nominations.

43. The Office of the High Commissioner for Human Rights shall immediately prepare, maintain and periodically update a public list of eligible candidates in a standardized format, which shall include personal data, areas of expertise and professional experience. Upcoming vacancies of mandates shall be publicized.

44. The principle of non-accumulation of human rights functions at a time shall be respected.

45. A mandate-holder's tenure in a given function, whether a thematic or country mandate, will be no longer than six years (two terms of three years for thematic mandate-holders).

46. Individuals holding decision-making positions in Government or in any other organization or entity which may give rise to a conflict of interest with the responsibilities inherent to the mandate shall be excluded. Mandate holders will act in their personal capacity.

47. A consultative group would be established to propose to the President, at least one month before the beginning of the session in which the Council would consider the selection of mandate holders, a list of candidates who possess the highest qualifications for the mandates in question and meet the general criteria and particular requirements.

48. The consultative group shall also give due consideration to the exclusion of nominated candidates from the public list of eligible candidates brought to its attention.

49. At the beginning of the annual cycle of the Council, Regional Groups would be invited to appoint a member of the consultative group, who would serve in his/her personal capacity. The Group will be assisted by the Office of the High Commissioner for Human Rights.

50. The consultative group will consider candidates included in the public list; however, under exceptional circumstances and if a particular post justifies it, the Group may consider additional nominations with equal or more suitable qualifications for the post. Recommendations to the President shall be public and substantiated.

51. The consultative group should take into account, as appropriate, the views of stakeholders, including the current or outgoing mandate-holders, in determining the necessary expertise, experience, skills, and other relevant requirements for each mandate.

52. On the basis of the recommendations of the consultative group and following broad consultations, in particular through the regional coordinators, the President of the Council will identify an appropriate candidate for each vacancy. The President will present to member States and observers a list of candidates to be proposed at least two weeks prior to the beginning of the session in which the Council will consider the appointments.

53. If necessary, the President will conduct further consultations to ensure the endorsement of the proposed candidates. The appointment of the special procedures mandate-holders will be completed upon the subsequent approval of the Council. Mandate-holders shall be appointed before the end of the session.

B. Review, rationalization and improvement of mandates

54. The review, rationalization and improvement of mandates, as well as the creation of new ones, must be guided by the principles of universality, impartiality, objectivity and non-selectivity, constructive international dialogue and cooperation, with a view to enhancing the promotion and protection of all human rights, civil, political, economic, social and cultural rights, including the right to development.

55. The review, rationalization and improvement of each mandate would take place in the context of the negotiations of the relevant resolutions. An assessment of the mandate may take place in a separate segment of the interactive dialogue between the Council and special procedures mandate-holders.

56. The review, rationalization and improvement of mandates would focus on the relevance, scope and contents of the mandates, having as a framework the internationally recognized human rights standards, the system of special procedures and General Assembly resolution 60/251.

57. Any decision to streamline, merge or possibly discontinue mandates should always be guided by the need for improvement of the enjoyment and protection of human rights.

58. The Council should always strive for improvements:

   (a) Mandates should always offer a clear prospect of an increased level of human rights protection and promotion as well as being coherent within the system of human rights;

   (b) Equal attention should be paid to all human rights. The balance of thematic mandates should broadly reflect the accepted equal importance of civil, political, economic, social and cultural rights, including the right to development;

(*c*) Every effort should be made to avoid unnecessary duplication;

(*d*) Areas which constitute thematic gaps will be identified and addressed, including by means other than the creation of special procedures mandates, such as by expanding an existing mandate, bringing a cross-cutting issue to the attention of mandate-holders or by requesting a joint action to the relevant mandate-holders;

(*e*) Any consideration of merging mandates should have regard to the content and predominant functions of each mandate, as well as to the workload of individual mandate-holders;

(*f*) In creating or reviewing mandates, efforts should be made to identify whether the structure of the mechanism (expert, rapporteur or working group) is the most effective in terms of increasing human rights protection;

(*g*) New mandates should be as clear and specific as possible, so as to avoid ambiguity.

59. It should be considered desirable to have a uniform nomenclature of mandate-holders, titles of mandates as well as a selection and appointment process, to make the whole system more understandable.

60. Thematic mandate periods will be of three years. Country mandate periods will be of one year.

61. Mandates included in Appendix I, where applicable, will be renewed until the date on which they are considered by the Council according to the programme of work.[d]

62. Current mandate-holders may continue serving, provided they have not exceeded the six-year term limit (Appendix II). On an exceptional basis, the term of those mandate-holders who have served more than six years may be extended until the relevant mandate is considered by the Council and the selection and appointment process has concluded.

63. Decisions to create, review or discontinue country mandates should also take into account the principles of cooperation and genuine dialogue aimed at strengthening the capacity of Member States to comply with their human rights obligations.

64. In case of situations of violations of human rights or a lack of cooperation that require the Council's attention, the principles of objectivity, non-selectivity, and the elimination of double standards and politicization should apply.

III. HUMAN RIGHTS COUNCIL ADVISORY COMMITTEE

65. The Human Rights Council Advisory Committee (hereinafter 'the Advisory Committee'), composed of 18 experts serving in their personal capacity, will function as a think-tank for the Council and work at its direction. The establishment of this subsidiary body and its functioning will be executed according to the guidelines stipulated below.

A. Nomination

66. All Member States of the United Nations may propose or endorse candidates from their own region. When selecting their candidates, States should consult their national

human rights institutions and civil society organizations and, in this regard, include the names of those supporting their candidates.

67. The aim is to ensure that the best possible expertise is made available to the Council. For this purpose, technical and objective requirements for the submission of candidatures will be established and approved by the Council at its sixth session (first session of the second cycle). These should include:

    (*a*) Recognized competence and experience in the field of human rights;

    (*b*) High moral standing;

    (*c*) Independence and impartiality.

68. Individuals holding decision-making positions in Government or in any other organization or entity which might give rise to a conflict of interest with the responsibilities inherent in the mandate shall be excluded. Elected members of the Committee will act in their personal capacity.

69. The principle of non-accumulation of human rights functions at the same time shall be respected.

B. Election

70. The Council shall elect the members of the Advisory Committee, in secret ballot, from the list of candidates whose names have been presented in accordance with the agreed requirements.

71. The list of candidates shall be closed two months prior to the election date. The Secretariat will make available the list of candidates and relevant information to member States and to the public at least one month prior to their election.

72. Due consideration should be given to gender balance and appropriate representation of different civilizations and legal systems.

73. The geographic distribution will be as follows:
    African States: 5
    Asian States: 5
    Eastern European States: 2
    Latin American and Caribbean States: 3
    Western European and other States: 3

74. The members of the Advisory Committee shall serve for a period of three years. They shall be eligible for re-election once. In the first term, one third of the experts will serve for one year and another third for two years. The staggering of terms of membership will be defined by the drawing of lots.

C. Functions

75. The function of the Advisory Committee is to provide expertise to the Council in the

manner and form requested by the Council, focusing mainly on studies and research-based advice. Further, such expertise shall be rendered only upon the latter's request, in compliance with its resolutions and under its guidance.

76. The Advisory Committee should be implementation-oriented and the scope of its advice should be limited to thematic issues pertaining to the mandate of the Council; namely promotion and protection of all human rights.

77. The Advisory Committee shall not adopt resolutions or decisions. The Advisory Committee may propose within the scope of the work set out by the Council, for the latter's consideration and approval, suggestions for further enhancing its procedural efficiency, as well as further research proposals within the scope of the work set out by the Council.

78. The Council shall issue specific guidelines for the Advisory Committee when it requests a substantive contribution from the latter and shall review all or any portion of those guidelines if it deems necessary in the future.

D. Methods of work

79. The Advisory Committee shall convene up to two sessions for a maximum of 10 working days per year. Additional sessions may be scheduled on an ad hoc basis with prior approval of the Council.

80. The Council may request the Advisory Committee to undertake certain tasks that could be performed collectively, through a smaller team or individually. The Advisory Committee will report on such efforts to the Council.

81. Members of the Advisory Committee are encouraged to communicate between sessions, individually or in teams. However, the Advisory Committee shall not establish subsidiary bodies unless the Council authorizes it to do so.

82. In the performance of its mandate, the Advisory Committee is urged to establish interaction with States, national human rights institutions, non-governmental organizations and other civil society entities in accordance with the modalities of the Council.

83. Member States and observers, including States that are not members of the Council, the specialized agencies, other intergovernmental organizations and national human rights institutions, as well as non-governmental organizations shall be entitled to participate in the work of the Advisory Committee based on arrangements, including Economic and Social Council resolution 1996/31 and practices observed by the Commission on Human Rights and the Council, while ensuring the most effective contribution of these entities.

84. The Council will decide at its sixth session (first session of its second cycle) on the most appropriate mechanisms to continue the work of the Working Groups on Indigenous Populations; Contemporary Forms of Slavery; Minorities; and the Social Forum.

IV. COMPLAINT PROCEDURE

A. Objective and scope

85. A complaint procedure is being established to address consistent patterns of gross and reliably attested violations of all human rights and all fundamental freedoms occurring in any part of the world and under any circumstances.

86. Economic and Social Council resolution 1503 (XLVIII) of 27 May 1970 as revised by resolution 2000/3 of 19 June 2000 served as a working basis and was improved where necessary, so as to ensure that the complaint procedure is impartial, objective, efficient, victims-oriented and conducted in a timely manner. The procedure will retain its confidential nature, with a view to enhancing cooperation with the State concerned.

B. Admissibility criteria for communications

87. A communication related to a violation of human rights and fundamental freedoms, for the purpose of this procedure, shall be admissible, provided that:

   (*a*) It is not manifestly politically motivated and its object is consistent with the Charter of the United Nations, the Universal Declaration of Human Rights and other applicable instruments in the field of human rights law;

   (*b*) It gives a factual description of the alleged violations, including the rights which are alleged to be violated;

   (*c*) Its language is not abusive. However, such a communication may be considered if it meets the other criteria for admissibility after deletion of the abusive language;

   (*d*) It is submitted by a person or a group of persons claiming to be the victims of violations of human rights and fundamental freedoms, or by any person or group of persons, including non-governmental organizations, acting in good faith in accordance with the principles of human rights, not resorting to politically motivated stands contrary to the provisions of the Charter of the United Nations and claiming to have direct and reliable knowledge of the violations concerned. Nonetheless, reliably attested communications shall not be inadmissible solely because the knowledge of the individual authors is second-hand, provided that they are accompanied by clear evidence;

   (*e*) It is not exclusively based on reports disseminated by mass media;

   (*f*) It does not refer to a case that appears to reveal a consistent pattern of gross and reliably attested violations of human rights already being dealt with by a special procedure, a treaty body or other United Nations or similar regional complaints procedure in the field of human rights;

   (*g*) Domestic remedies have been exhausted, unless it appears that such remedies would be ineffective or unreasonably prolonged.

88. National human rights institutions, established and operating under the Principles Relating to the Status of National Institutions (the Paris Principles), in particular in regard to quasi-judicial competence, may serve as effective means of addressing individual human rights violations.

C. Working groups

89. Two distinct working groups shall be established with the mandate to examine the communications and to bring to the attention of the Council consistent patterns of gross and reliably attested violations of human rights and fundamental freedoms.

90. Both working groups shall, to the greatest possible extent, work on the basis of consensus. In the absence of consensus, decisions shall be taken by simple majority of the votes. They may establish their own rules of procedure.

1. Working Group on Communications: composition, mandate and powers

91. The Human Rights Council Advisory Committee shall appoint five of its members, one from each Regional Group, with due consideration to gender balance, to constitute the Working Group on Communications.

92. In case of a vacancy, the Advisory Committee shall appoint an independent and highly qualified expert of the same Regional Group from the Advisory Committee.

93. Since there is a need for independent expertise and continuity with regard to the examination and assessment of communications received, the independent and highly qualified experts of the Working Group on Communications shall be appointed for three years. Their mandate is renewable only once.

94. The Chairperson of the Working Group on Communications is requested, together with the secretariat, to undertake an initial screening of communications received, based on the admissibility criteria, before transmitting them to the States concerned. Manifestly ill-founded or anonymous communications shall be screened out by the Chairperson and shall therefore not be transmitted to the State concerned. In a perspective of accountability and transparency, the Chairperson of the Working Group on Communications shall provide all its members with a list of all communications rejected after initial screening. This list should indicate the grounds of all decisions resulting in the rejection of a communication. All other communications, which have not been screened out, shall be transmitted to the State concerned, so as to obtain the views of the latter on the allegations of violations.

95. The members of the Working Group on Communications shall decide on the admissibility of a communication and assess the merits of the allegations of violations, including whether the communication alone or in combination with other communications appear to reveal a consistent pattern of gross and reliably attested violations of human rights and fundamental freedoms. The Working Group on Communications shall provide the Working Group on Situations with a file containing all admissible communications as well as recommendations thereon. When the Working Group on Communications requires further consideration or additional information, it may keep a case under review until its next session and request such information from the State concerned. The Working Group on Communications may decide to dismiss a case. All decisions of the Working Group on Communications shall be based on a rigorous application of the admissibility criteria and duly justified.

2. Working Group on Situations: composition, mandate and powers

96. Each Regional Group shall appoint a representative of a member State of the Council, with due consideration to gender balance, to serve on the Working Group on Situations. Members shall be appointed for one year. Their mandate may be renewed once, if the State concerned is a member of the Council.

97. Members of the Working Group on Situations shall serve in their personal capacity. In order to fill a vacancy, the respective Regional Group to which the vacancy belongs, shall appoint a representative from member States of the same Regional Group.

98. The Working Group on Situations is requested, on the basis of the information and recommendations provided by the Working Group on Communications, to present the Council with a report on consistent patterns of gross and reliably attested violations of human rights and fundamental freedoms and to make recommendations to the Council on the course of action to take, normally in the form of a draft resolution or decision with respect to the situations referred to it. When the Working Group on Situations requires further consideration or additional information, its members may keep a case under review until its next session. The Working Group on Situations may also decide to dismiss a case.

99. All decisions of the Working Group on Situations shall be duly justified and indicate why the consideration of a situation has been discontinued or action recommended thereon. Decisions to discontinue should be taken by consensus; if that is not possible, by simple majority of the votes.

D. Working modalities and confidentiality

100. Since the complaint procedure is to be, inter alia, victims-oriented and conducted in a confidential and timely manner, both Working Groups shall meet at least twice a year for five working days each session, in order to promptly examine the communications received, including replies of States thereon, and the situations of which the Council is already seized under the complaint procedure.

101. The State concerned shall cooperate with the complaint procedure and make every effort to provide substantive replies in one of the United Nations official languages to any of the requests of the Working Groups or the Council. The State concerned shall also make every effort to provide a reply not later than three months after the request has been made. If necessary, this deadline may however be extended at the request of the State concerned.

102. The Secretariat is requested to make the confidential files available to all members of the Council, at least two weeks in advance, so as to allow sufficient time for the consideration of the files.

103. The Council shall consider consistent patterns of gross and reliably attested violations of human rights and fundamental freedoms brought to its attention by the Working Group on Situations as frequently as needed, but at least once a year.

104. The reports of the Working Group on Situations referred to the Council shall be exam-

ined in a confidential manner, unless the Council decides otherwise. When the Working Group on Situations recommends to the Council that it consider a situation in a public meeting, in particular in the case of manifest and unequivocal lack of cooperation, the Council shall consider such recommendation on a priority basis at its next session.

105. So as to ensure that the complaint procedure is victims-oriented, efficient and conducted in a timely manner, the period of time between the transmission of the complaint to the State concerned and consideration by the Council shall not, in principle, exceed 24 months.

E. Involvement of the complainant and of the State concerned

106. The complaint procedure shall ensure that both the author of a communication and the State concerned are informed of the proceedings at the following key stages:

(*a*) When a communication is deemed inadmissible by the Working Group on Communications or when it is taken up for consideration by the Working Group on Situations; or when a communication is kept pending by one of the Working Groups or by the Council;

(*b*) At the final outcome.

107. In addition, the complainant shall be informed when his/her communication is registered by the complaint procedure.

108. Should the complainant request that his/her identity be kept confidential, it will not be transmitted to the State concerned.

F. Measures

109. In accordance with established practice the action taken in respect of a particular situation should be one of the following options:

(*a*) To discontinue considering the situation when further consideration or action is not warranted;

(*b*) To keep the situation under review and request the State concerned to provide further information within a reasonable period of time;

(*c*) To keep the situation under review and appoint an independent and highly qualified expert to monitor the situation and report back to the Council;

(*d*) To discontinue reviewing the matter under the confidential complaint procedure in order to take up public consideration of the same;

(*e*) To recommend to OHCHR to provide technical cooperation, capacity-building assistance or advisory services to the State concerned.

V. AGENDA AND FRAMEWORK FOR THE PROGRAMME OF WORK

A. Principles

Universality

Impartiality

Objectivity

Non-selectiveness

Constructive dialogue and cooperation

Predictability

Flexibility

Transparency

Accountability

Balance

Inclusive/comprehensive

Gender perspective

Implementation and follow-up of decisions

B. Agenda

Item 1. Organizational and procedural matters

Item 2. Annual report of the United Nations High Commissioner for Human Rights and reports of the Office of the High Commissioner and the Secretary-General

Item 3. Promotion and protection of all human rights, civil, political, economic, social and cultural rights, including the right to development

Item 4. Human rights situations that require the Council's attention

Item 5. Human rights bodies and mechanisms

Item 6. Universal Periodic Review

Item 7. Human rights situation in Palestine and other occupied Arab territories

Item 8. Follow-up and implementation of the Vienna Declaration and Programme of Action

Item 9. Racism, racial discrimination, xenophobia and related forms of intolerance, follow-up and implementation of the Durban Declaration and Programme of Action

Item 10. Technical assistance and capacity-building

C. Framework for the programme of work

Item 1. Organizational and procedural matters

Election of the Bureau

Adoption of the annual programme of work

Adoption of the programme of work of the session, including other business

Selection and appointment of mandate-holders

Election of members of the Human Rights Council Advisory Committee

Adoption of the report of the session

Adoption of the annual report

Item 2. Annual report of the United Nations High Commissioner for Human Rights and reports of the Office of the High Commissioner and the Secretary-General

Presentation of the annual report and updates

Item 3. Promotion and protection of all human rights, civil, political, economic, social and cultural rights, including the right to development

Economic, social and cultural rights

Civil and political rights

Rights of peoples, and specific groups and individuals

Right to development

Interrelation of human rights and human rights thematic issues

Item 4. Human rights situations that require the Council's attention

Item 5. Human rights bodies and mechanisms

Report of the Human Rights Council Advisory Committee

Report of the complaint procedure

Item 6. Universal Periodic Review

Item 7. Human rights situation in Palestine and other occupied Arab territories

Human rights violations and implications of the Israeli occupation of Palestine and other occupied Arab territories

Right to self-determination of the Palestinian people

Item 8. Follow-up and implementation of the Vienna Declaration and Programme of Action

Item 9. Racism, racial discrimination, xenophobia and related forms of intolerance, follow-up and implementation of the Durban Declaration and Programme of Action

Item 10. Technical assistance and capacity-building

VI. METHODS OF WORK

110. The methods of work, pursuant to General Assembly resolution 60/251 should be transparent, impartial, equitable, fair, pragmatic; lead to clarity, predictability, and inclusiveness. They may also be updated and adjusted over time.

A. Institutional arrangements

1. Briefings on prospective resolutions or decisions

111. The briefings on prospective resolutions or decisions would be informative only, whereby delegations would be apprised of resolutions and/or decisions tabled or intended to be tabled. These briefings will be organized by interested delegations.

2. President's open-ended information meetings on resolutions, decisions and other related business

112. The President's open-ended information meetings on resolutions, decisions and other related business shall provide information on the status of negotiations on draft resolutions and/or decisions so that delegations may gain a bird's eye view of the status of such drafts. The consultations shall have a purely informational function, combined with information on the extranet, and be held in a transparent and inclusive manner. They shall not serve as a negotiating forum.

3. Informal consultations on proposals convened by main sponsors

113. Informal consultations shall be the primary means for the negotiation of draft resolutions and/or decisions, and their convening shall be the responsibility of the sponsor(s). At least one informal open-ended consultation should be held on each draft resolution and/or decision before it is considered for action by the Council. Consultations should, as much as possible, be scheduled in a timely, transparent and inclusive manner that takes into account the constraints faced by delegations, particularly smaller ones.

4. Role of the Bureau

114. The Bureau shall deal with procedural and organizational matters. The Bureau shall regularly communicate the contents of its meetings through a timely summary report.

5. Other work formats may include panel debates, seminars and round tables

115. Utilization of these other work formats, including topics and modalities, would be decided by the Council on a case-by-case basis. They may serve as tools of the Council for enhancing dialogue and mutual understanding on certain issues. They should be utilized in the context of the Council's agenda and annual programme of work, and reinforce and/or complement its intergovernmental nature. They shall not be used to substitute or replace existing human rights mechanisms and established methods of work.

6. High-Level Segment

116. The High-Level Segment shall be held once a year during the main session of the Council. It shall be followed by a general segment wherein delegations that did not participate in the High-Level Segment may deliver general statements.

B. Working culture

117. There is a need for:

(*a*) Early notification of proposals;

(*b*) Early submission of draft resolutions and decisions, preferably by the end of the penultimate week of a session;

(*c*) Early distribution of all reports, particularly those of special procedures, to be transmitted to delegations in a timely fashion, at least 15 days in advance of their consideration by the Council, and in all official United Nations languages;

(*d*) Proposers of a country resolution to have the responsibility to secure the broadest possible support for their initiatives (preferably 15 members), before action is taken;

(*e*) Restraint in resorting to resolutions, in order to avoid proliferation of resolutions without prejudice to the right of States to decide on the periodicity of presenting their draft proposals by:

  (i)   Minimizing unnecessary duplication of initiatives with the General Assembly/Third Committee;

  (ii) Clustering of agenda items;

  (iii) Staggering the tabling of decisions and/or resolutions and consideration of action on agenda items/issues.

C. Outcomes other than resolutions and decisions

118. These may include recommendations, conclusions, summaries of discussions and President's Statement. As such outcomes would have different legal implications, they should supplement and not replace resolutions and decisions.

D. Special sessions of the Council

119. The following provisions shall complement the general framework provided by General Assembly resolution 60/251 and the rules of procedure of the Human Rights Council.

120. The rules of procedure of special sessions shall be in accordance with the rules of procedure applicable for regular sessions of the Council.

121. The request for the holding of a special session, in accordance with the requirement established in paragraph 10 of General Assembly resolution 60/251, shall be submitted to the President and to the secretariat of the Council. The request shall specify the item proposed for consideration and include any other relevant information the sponsors may wish to provide.

122. The special session shall be convened as soon as possible after the formal request is communicated, but, in principle, not earlier than two working days, and not later than five working days after the formal receipt of the request. The duration of the special session shall not exceed three days (six working sessions), unless the Council decides otherwise.

123. The secretariat of the Council shall immediately communicate the request for the holding of a special session and any additional information provided by the sponsors in the request, as well as the date for the convening of the special session, to all United Nations Member States and make the information available to the specialized agencies, other intergovernmental organizations and national human rights institutions, as well as to non-governmental organizations in consultative status by the most expedient and expeditious means of communication. Special session documentation, in particular draft resolutions and decisions, should be made available in all official United Nations languages to all States in an equitable, timely and transparent manner.

124. The President of the Council should hold open-ended informative consultations before the special session on its conduct and organization. In this regard, the secretariat may also be requested to provide additional information, including, on the methods of work of previous special sessions.

125. Members of the Council, concerned States, observer States, specialized agencies, other intergovernmental organizations and national human rights institutions, as well as non-governmental organizations in consultative status may contribute to the special session in accordance with the rules of procedure of the Council.

126. If the requesting or other States intend to present draft resolutions or decisions at the special session, texts should be made available in accordance with the Council's relevant rules of procedure. Nevertheless, sponsors are urged to present such texts as early as possible.

127. The sponsors of a draft resolution or decision should hold open-ended consultations on the text of their draft resolution(s) or decision(s) with a view to achieving the widest participation in their consideration and, if possible, achieving consensus on them.

128. A special session should allow participatory debate, be results-oriented and geared to achieving practical outcomes, the implementation of which can be monitored and reported on at the following regular session of the Council for possible follow-up decision.

VII. RULES OF PROCEDURE[e]

SESSIONS

Rules of procedure

Rule 1

The Human Rights Council shall apply the rules of procedure established for the Main Committees of the General Assembly, as applicable, unless subsequently otherwise decided by the Assembly or the Council.

REGULAR SESSIONS

Number of sessions

Rule 2

The Human Rights Council shall meet regularly throughout the year and schedule no fewer than three sessions per Council year, including a main session, for a total duration of no less than 10 weeks.

Assumption of membership

Rule 3

Newly-elected member States of the Human Rights Council shall assume their membership on the first day of the Council year, replacing member States that have concluded their respective membership terms.

Place of meeting

Rule 4

The Human Rights Council shall be based in Geneva.

SPECIAL SESSIONS

Convening of special sessions

Rule 5

The rules of procedure of special sessions of the Human Rights Council will be the same as the rules of procedure applicable for regular sessions of the Human Rights Council.

Rule 6

The Human Rights Council shall hold special sessions, when needed, at the request of a member of the Council with the support of one third of the membership of the Council.

PARTICIPATION OF AND CONSULTATION WITH OBSERVERS OF THE COUNCIL

Rule 7

(*a*) The Council shall apply the rules of procedure established for committees of the General Assembly, as applicable, unless subsequently otherwise decided by the Assembly or the Council, and the participation of and consultation with observers, including States that are not members of the Council, the specialized agencies, other intergovernmental organizations and national human rights institutions, as well as non-governmental organizations, shall be based on arrangements, including Economic and Social Council resolution 1996/31 of 25 July 1996, and practices observed by the Commission on Human Rights, while ensuring the most effective contribution of these entities.

(*b*) Participation of national human rights institutions shall be based on arrangements and practices agreed upon by the Commission on Human Rights, including resolution 2005/74 of 20 April 2005, while ensuring the most effective contribution of these entities.

ORGANIZATION OF WORK AND AGENDA FOR REGULAR SESSIONS

Organizational meetings

Rule 8

(*a*) At the beginning of each Council year, the Council shall hold an organizational meeting to elect its Bureau and to consider and adopt the agenda, programme of work, and calendar of regular sessions for the Council year indicating, if possible, a target date for the conclusion of its work, the approximate dates of consideration of items and the number of meetings to be allocated to each item.

(*b*) The President of the Council shall also convene organizational meetings two weeks before the beginning of each session and, if necessary, during the Council sessions to discuss organizational and procedural issues pertinent to that session.

PRESIDENT AND VICE-PRESIDENTS

Elections

Rule 9

(*a*) At the beginning of each Council year, at its organizational meeting, the Council shall elect, from among the representatives of its members, a President and four Vice-Presidents. The President and the Vice Presidents shall constitute the Bureau. One of the Vice-Presidents shall serve as Rapporteur.

(*b*) In the election of the President of the Council, regard shall be had for the equitable geographical rotation of this office among the following Regional Groups: African States, Asian States, Eastern European States, Latin American and Caribbean States, and Western European and other States. The four Vice-Presidents of the Council shall be elected on the basis of equitable geographical distribution from the Regional Groups other than the one to which the President belongs. The selection of the Rapporteur shall be based on geographic rotation.

Bureau

Rule 10

The Bureau shall deal with procedural and organizational matters.

Term of office

Rule 11

The President and the Vice-Presidents shall, subject to rule 13, hold office for a period of one year. They shall not be eligible for immediate re-election to the same post.

Absence of officers

Rule 12 [105]

If the President finds it necessary to be absent during a meeting or any part thereof, he/she shall designate one of the Vice-Presidents to take his/her place. A Vice-President acting as President shall have the same powers and duties as the President. If the President ceases to hold office pursuant to rule 13, the remaining members of the Bureau shall designate one of the Vice-Presidents to take his/her place until the election of a new President.

Replacement of the President or a Vice-President

Rule 13

If the President or any Vice-President ceases to be able to carry out his/her functions or ceases to be a representative of a member of the Council, or if the Member of the United Nations of which he/she is a representative ceases to be a member of the Council, he/she shall cease to hold such office and a new President or Vice-President shall be elected for the unexpired term.

SECRETARIAT

Duties of the secretariat

Rule 14 [47]

The Office of the United Nations High Commissioner for Human Rights shall act as secretariat for the Council. In this regard, it shall receive, translate, print and circulate in all official United Nations languages, documents, reports and resolutions of the Council, its committees and its organs; interpret speeches made at the meetings; prepare, print and circulate the records of the session; have the custody and proper preservation of the documents in the archives of the Council; distribute all documents of the Council to the members of the Council and observers and, generally, perform all other support functions which the Council may require.

RECORDS AND REPORT

Report to the General Assembly

Rule 15

The Council shall submit an annual report to the General Assembly.

PUBLIC AND PRIVATE MEETINGS OF THE HUMAN RIGHTS COUNCIL

General principles

Rule 16 [60]

The meetings of the Council shall be held in public unless the Council decides that exceptional circumstances require the meeting be held in private.

Private meetings

Rule 17 [61]

All decisions of the Council taken at a private meeting shall be announced at an early public meeting of the Council.

CONDUCT OF BUSINESS

Working groups and other arrangements

Rule 18

The Council may set up working groups and other arrangements. Participation in these bodies shall be decided upon by the members, based on rule 7. The rules of procedure of these bodies shall follow those of the Council, as applicable, unless decided otherwise by the Council.

Quorum

Rule 19 [67]

The President may declare a meeting open and permit the debate to proceed when at least one third of the members of the Council are present. The presence of a majority of the members shall be required for any decision to be taken.

Majority required

Rule 20 [125]

Decisions of the Council shall be made by a simple majority of the members present and voting, subject to rule 19.

Appendix I

RENEWED MANDATES UNTIL THEY COULD BE CONSIDERED BY THE HUMAN RIGHTS COUNCIL ACCORDING TO ITS ANNUAL PROGRAMME OF WORK

Independent expert appointed by the Secretary-General on the situation of human rights in Haiti

Independent expert appointed by the Secretary-General on the situation of human rights in Somalia

Independent expert on the situation of human rights in Burundi

Independent expert on technical cooperation and advisory services in Liberia

Independent expert on the situation of human rights in the Democratic Republic of the Congo

Independent expert on human rights and international solidarity

Independent expert on minority issues

Independent expert on the effects of economic reform policies and foreign debt on the full enjoyment of all human rights, particularly economic, social and cultural rights

Independent expert on the question of human rights and extreme poverty

Special Rapporteur on the situation of human rights in the Sudan

Special Rapporteur on the situation of human rights in Myanmar

Special Rapporteur on the situation of human rights in the Democratic People's Republic of Korea

Special Rapporteur on the situation of human rights in the Palestinian territories occupied since 1967 (The duration of this mandate has been established until the end of the occupation.)

Special Rapporteur on adequate housing as a component of the right to an adequate standard of living

Special Rapporteur on contemporary forms of racism, racial discrimination, xenophobia and related intolerance

Special Rapporteur on extrajudicial, summary or arbitrary executions

Special Rapporteur on freedom of religion or belief

Special Rapporteur on the adverse effects of the illicit movement and dumping of toxic and dangerous products and wastes on the enjoyment of human rights

Special Rapporteur on the human rights aspects of the victims of trafficking in persons, especially women and children

Special Rapporteur on the human rights of migrants

Special Rapporteur on the independence of judges and lawyers

Special Rapporteur on the promotion and protection of human rights and fundamental freedoms while countering terrorism

Special Rapporteur on the promotion and protection of the right to freedom of opinion and expression

Special Rapporteur on the right of everyone to the enjoyment of the highest attainable standard of physical and mental health

Special Rapporteur on the right to education

Special Rapporteur on the right to food

Special Rapporteur on the sale of children, child prostitution and child pornography

Special Rapporteur on the situation of human rights and fundamental freedoms of indigenous people

Special Rapporteur on torture and other cruel, inhuman or degrading treatment or punishment

Special Rapporteur on violence against women, its causes and consequences

Special Representative of the Secretary-General on the issue of human rights and transnational corporations and other business enterprises

Special Representative of the Secretary-General for human rights in Cambodia

Special Representative of the Secretary-General on the situation of human rights defenders

Representative of the Secretary-General on human rights of internally displaced persons

Working Group of Experts on People of African Descent

Working Group on Arbitrary Detention

Working Group on Enforced or Involuntary Disappearances

Working Group on the question of the use of mercenaries as a means of violating human rights and impeding the exercise of the right of peoples to self-determination

Appendix II

TERMS IN OFFICE OF MANDATE-HOLDERS

Mandate-holder	Mandate	Terms in office
Charlotte Abaka	Independent Expert on the situation of human rights in Liberia	July 2006 (first term)
Yakin Ertürk	Special Rapporteur on violence against women, its causes and consequences	July 2006 (first term)
Manuela Carmena Castrillo	Working Group on Arbitrary Detention	July 2006 (first term)
Joel Adebayo Adekanye	Working Group on Enforced or Involuntary Disappearances	July 2006 (second term)
Saeed Rajaee Khorasani	Working Group on Enforced or Involuntary Disappearances	July 2006 (first term)
Joe Frans	Working Group on people of African descent	July 2006 (first term)
Leandro Despouy	Special Rapporteur on the independence of judges and lawyers	August 2006 (first term)
Hina Jilani	Special Representative of the Secretary-General on the situation of human rights defenders	August 2006 (second term)
Soledad Villagra de Biedermann	Working Group on Arbitrary Detention	August 2006 (second term)
Miloon Kothari	Special Rapporteur on adequate housing as a component of the right to an adequate standard of living	September 2006 (second term)
Jean Ziegler	Special Rapporteur on the right to food	September 2006 (second term)
Paulo Sérgio Pinheiro	Special Rapporteur on the situation of human rights in Myanmar	December 2006 (second term)
Darko Göttlicher	Working Group on Enforced or Involuntary Disappearances	January 2007 (first term)
Tamás Bán	Working Group on Arbitrary Detention	April 2007 (second term)
Ghanim Alnajjar	Independent Expert appointed by the Secretary-General on the situation of human rights in Somalia	May 2007 (second term)

John Dugard	Special Rapporteur on the situation of human rights in the Palestinian territories occupied since 1967	June 2007 (second term)
Rodolfo Stavenhagen	Special Rapporteur on the situation of human rights and fundamental freedoms of indigenous people	June 2007 (second term)
Arjun Sengupta	Independent Expert on the question of human rights and extreme poverty	July 2007 (first term)
Akich Okola	Independent Expert on the situation of human rights in Burundi	July 2007 (first term)
Titinga Frédéric Pacéré	Independent Expert on the situation of human rights in the Democratic Republic of the Congo	July 2007 (first term)
Philip Alston	Special Rapporteur on extrajudicial, summary or arbitrary executions	July 2007 (first term)
Asma Jahangir	Special Rapporteur on freedom of religion or belief	July 2007 (first term)
Okechukwu Ibeanu	Special Rapporteur on the adverse effects of the illicit movement and dumping of toxic and dangerous products and wastes on the enjoyment of human rights	July 2007 (first term)
Vernor Muñoz Villalobos	Special Rapporteur on the right to education	July 2007 (first term)
Juan Miguel Petit	Special Rapporteur on the sale of children, child prostitution and child pornography	July 2007 (second term)
Vitit Muntarbhorn	Special Rapporteur on the situation of human rights in the Democratic People's Republic of Korea	July 2007 (first term)
Leila Zerrougui	Working Group on Arbitrary Detention	August 2007 (second term)
Santiago Corcuera Cabezut	Working Group on Enforced or Involuntary Disappearances	August 2007 (first term)
Walter Kälin	Representative of the Secretary-General on the human rights of internally displaced persons	September 2007 (first term)
Sigma Huda	Special Rapporteur on trafficking in persons, especially in women and children	October 2007 (first term)

Bernards Andrew Nyamwaya Mudho	Independent Expert on the effects of economic reform policies and foreign debt on the full enjoyment of human rights, particularly economic, social and cultural rights	November 2007 (second term)
Manfred Nowak	Special Rapporteur on torture and other cruel, inhuman or degrading treatment or punishment	November 2007 (first term)
Louis Joinet	Independent Expert appointed by the Secretary-General on the situation of human rights in Haiti	February 2008 (second term)
Rudi Muhammad Rizki	Independent Expert on human rights and international solidarity	July 2008 (first term)
Gay McDougall	Independent Expert on minority issues	July 2008 (first term)
Doudou Diène	Special Rapporteur on contemporary forms of racism, racial discrimination, xenophobia and related intolerance	July 2008 (second term)
Jorge A Bustamante	Special Rapporteur on the human rights of migrants	July 2008 (first term)
Martin Scheinin	Special Rapporteur on the promotion and protection of human rights while countering terrorism	July 2008 (first term)
Sima Samar	Special Rapporteur on the situation of human rights in the Sudan	July 2008 (first term)
John Ruggie	Special Representative of the Secretary-General on human rights and trans-national corporations and other business enterprises	July 2008 (first term)
Seyyed Mohammad Hashemi	Working Group on Arbitrary Detention	July 2008 (second term)
Najat Al-Hajjaji	Working Group on the use of mercenaries as a means of impeding the exercise of the right of peoples to self-determination	July 2008 (first term)
Amada Benavides de Pérez	Working Group on the use of mercenaries as a means of impeding the exercise of the right of peoples to self-determination	July 2008 (first term)

Alexander Ivanovich Nikitin	Working Group on the use of mercenaries as a means of impeding the exercise of the right of peoples to self-determination	July 2008 (first term)
Shaista Shameem	Working Group on the use of mercenaries as a means of impeding the exercise of the right of peoples to self-determination	July 2007 (first term)
Ambeyi Ligabo	Special Rapporteur on the promotion and protection of the right to freedom of opinion and expression	August 2008 (second term)
Paul Hunt	Special Rapporteur on the right of everyone to the enjoyment of the highest attainable standard of physical and mental health	August 2008 (second term)
Peter Lesa Kasanda	Working Group on people of African descent	August 2008 (second term)
Stephen J Toope	Working Group on Enforced or Involuntary Disappearances	September 2008 (second term)
George N Jabbour	Working Group on people of African descent	September 2008 (second term)
Irina Zlatescu	Working Group on people of African descent	October 2008 (second term)
José Gómez del Prado	Working Group on the use of mercenaries as a means of impeding the exercise of the right of peoples to self-determination	October 2008 (first term)
Yash Ghai	Special Representative of the Secretary-General for human rights in Cambodia	November 2008 (first term)

Notes

a   The universal periodic review is an evolving process; the Council, after the conclusion of the first review cycle, may review the modalities and the periodicity of this mechanism, based on best practices and lessons learned.

b   A Universal Periodic Review Voluntary Trust Fund should be established to facilitate the participation of developing countries, particularly the Least Developed Countries, in the universal periodic review mechanism.

c   A decision should be taken by the Council on whether to resort to existing financing mechanisms or to create a new mechanism.

d   Country mandates meet the following criteria:
   •   There is a pending mandate of the Council to be accomplished; or
   •   There is a pending mandate of the General Assembly to be accomplished; or
   •   The nature of the mandate is for advisory services and technical assistance.

e   Figures indicated in square brackets refer to identical or corresponding rules of the General Assembly or its Main Committees (A/520/Rev. 16).

Annex 2

General Guidelines for the Preparation of Information under the UPR*

HUMAN RIGHTS COUNCIL
Sixth session
Agenda items 1, 5 and 6

ORGANIZATIONAL AND PROCEDURAL MATTERS

HUMAN RIGHTS BODIES AND MECHANISMS

UNIVERSAL PERIODIC REVIEW

Follow-up to Human Rights Council resolution 5/1: draft decision submitted by the President

At its ... meeting, on ... September 2007, the Human Rights Council adopted, without a vote:

I.   GENERAL GUIDELINES FOR THE PREPARATION OF INFORMATION UNDER THE UNIVERSAL PERIODIC REVIEW

Reaffirming the relevant provisions, related to the universal periodic review, of General Assembly resolution 60/251 of 15 March 2006 and of Human Rights Council resolution 5/1 of 18 June 2007 containing the institution-building package, the Council adopts the following General Guidelines:

A.   Description of the methodology and the broad consultation process followed for the preparation of information provided under the universal periodic review;

B.   Background of the country under review and framework, particularly normative and institutional framework, for the promotion and protection of human rights: constitution, legislation, policy measures, national jurisprudence, human rights infrastructure including national human rights institutions and scope of international obligations identified in the 'basis of review' in resolution 5/1, annex, section IA;

C.   Promotion and protection of human rights on the ground: implementation of international human rights obligations identified in the 'basis of review'

---

*UN document. Please see: http://ap.ohchr.org/documents/E/HRC/decisions/A_HRC_DEC_6_102.pdf

in resolution 5/1, annex, section IA, national legislation and voluntary commitments, national human rights institutions activities, public awareness of human rights, cooperation with human rights mechanisms …;

D. Identification of achievements, best practices, challenges and constraints;

E. Key national priorities, initiatives and commitments that the State concerned intends to undertake to overcome those challenges and constraints and improve human rights situations on the ground;

F. Expectations of the State concerned in terms of capacity-building and requests, if any, for technical assistance;

G. Presentation by the State concerned of the follow-up to the previous review.

II. TECHNICAL AND OBJECTIVE REQUIREMENTS FOR ELIGIBLE CANDIDATES FOR MANDATE HOLDERS

A. Background

According to resolution 5/1, 'the following general criteria will be of paramount importance while nominating, selecting and appointing mandate holders: (*a*) expertise; (*b*) experience in the field of the mandate; (*c*) independency; (*d*) impartiality; (*e*) personal integrity; (*f*) objectivity'. Due consideration should be given to gender balance as well as to appropriate representation of different legal systems. 'Eligible candidates are highly qualified individuals who possess established competence, relevant expertise and extensive professional experience in the field of human rights' (paras 39–41).

B. General aspects

1. The Office of the United Nations High Commissioner for Human Rights has the responsibility to 'immediately prepare, maintain and periodically update a public list of eligible candidates in a standardized format'. The list shall include 'personal data, areas of expertise and professional experience' (resolution 5/1, para. 43).

2. The Secretariat may provide a standardized form, on the basis of the technical and objective requirements stipulated below, for candidates to fill in, and shall allow for highlighting any expertise they possess in specific areas, so as to facilitate the selection of relevant candidacies from the roster as soon as appointments for particular mandates are necessary.

3. The data and information provided by the candidates shall be substantiated by appropriate written credentials to be annexed to the curricula vitae.

4. 'A consultative group would be established to propose to the President, at least one month before the beginning of the session in which the Council would consider the selection of mandate holders, a list of candidates who possess the highest qualifications for the mandates in question and meet the general criteria and practical requirements' (resolution 5/1, para. 47).

C. Technical and objective requirements

The following should be considered:

1. Qualifications: relevant educational qualifications or equivalent professional experience in the field of human rights; good communication skills in one of the official languages of the United Nations.

2. Relevant expertise: knowledge of international human rights instruments, norms and principles; as well as knowledge of institutional mandates related to the United Nations or other international or regional organizations' work in the area of human rights; proven work experience in the field of human rights.

3. Established competence: nationally, regionally or internationally recognized competence related to human rights.

4. Flexibility/readiness and availability of time to perform effectively the functions of the mandate and to respond to its requirements, including attending Human Rights Council sessions.

III. ADVISORY COMMITTEE OF THE HUMAN RIGHTS COUNCIL

Technical and objective requirements for the submission of candidatures

Mandate: In conformity with resolution 5/1, the technical and objective requirements for the submission of candidatures will be established and approved by the Human Rights Council at its sixth session (first session of the second cycle). These should include:

– Recognized competence and experience in the field of human rights;

– High moral standing;

– Independence and impartiality.

When selecting their candidates, States should consult their national human rights institutions and civil society organizations and apply the following guidelines on technical and objective requirements for the submission of their candidates:

A.   Competence and experience

- Academic studies in the field of human rights or related areas and/or experience and exposure to leadership roles in the human rights field at the national, regional, or international level;

- Substantial experience (at least five years) and personal contributions in the field of human rights;

- Knowledge of the United Nations system and of institutional mandates and policies related to the work in the area of human rights, as well as knowledge of international human rights instruments, norms, disciplines, and familiarity with different legal systems and civilizations will be preferable;

- Proficiency in at least one of the United Nations official languages;

- Availability of time to fulfil the work of the Advisory Committee in an effective manner, both to attend its sessions and to carry out mandated activities between sessions.

B.   High moral standing

[...]

C.   Independence and impartiality

Individuals holding decision-making positions in Government or any other organization or entity which might give rise to a conflict of interest with responsibilities inherent to the mandate shall be excluded. Elected members of the Advisory Committee will act in their personal capacity.

D.   Other considerations

The principle of non-accumulation of human rights functions at the same time shall be respected.

In electing members of the Advisory Committee, the Council should give due consideration to gender balance and appropriate representation of different civilizations and legal systems.

Annex 3

Guide to Best Practice Flowchart

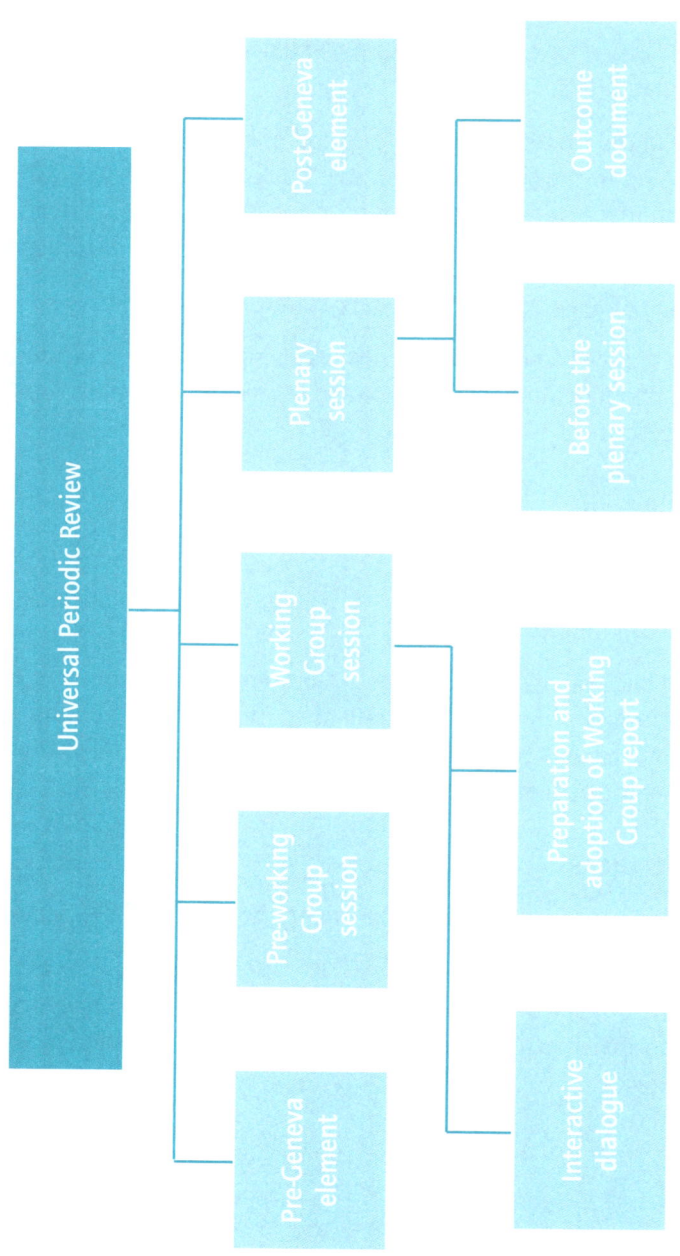

Universal Periodic Review

- Pre-Geneva element
- Pre-working Group session
- Working Group session
  - Interactive dialogue
  - Preparation and adoption of Working Group report
- Plenary session
  - Before the plenary session
  - Outcome document
- Post-Geneva element

PRE-GENEVA ELEMENT

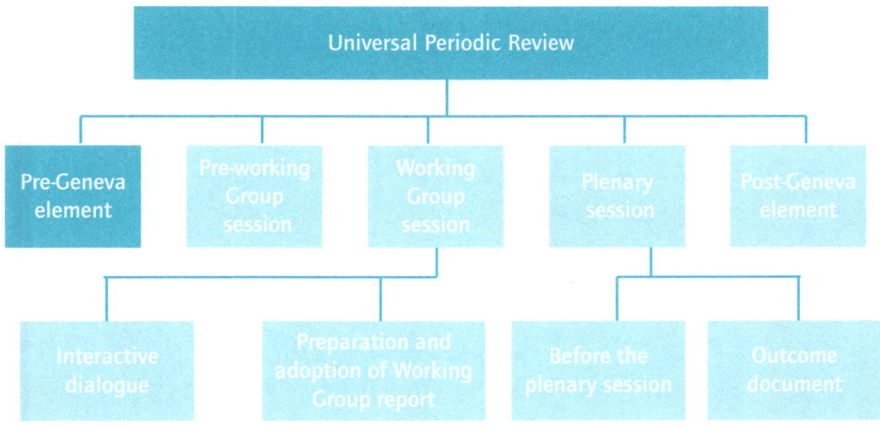

In line with Resolution 5/1, states to hold broad national consultations with all relevant stakeholders.

Stakeholders (NHRIs/CSOs) are encouraged to produce report/s. Information from stakeholder submissions will form part of the basis for the review.

Stakeholders to submit reports to HRC Secretariat six months prior to date of review in Geneva.

SuR to submit report to HRC Secretariat 12–14 weeks prior to date of review in Geneva.

If applicable, SuR to begin liaising with their diplomatic missions in Geneva.

SuR to co-ordinate with their troikas to co-ordinate for the preparation of the review.

PRE-WORKING GROUP SESSION

Before the interactive dialogue in Geneva

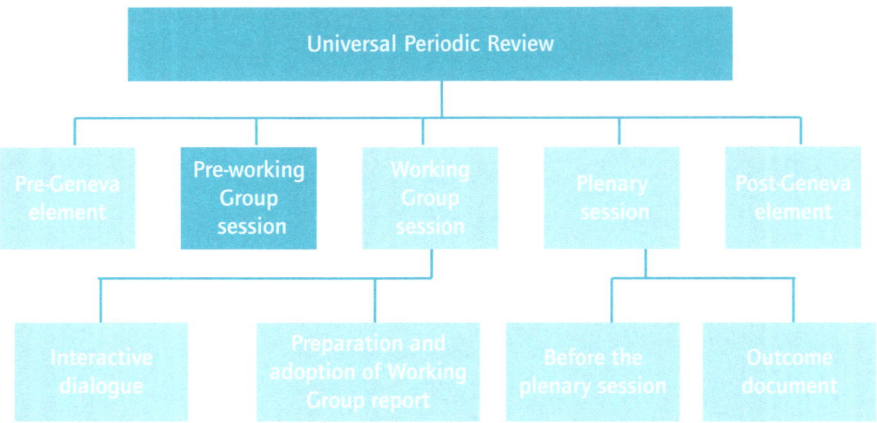

States that wish to submit questions/issues to the SuR before the interactive dialogue may do so via the troika. The troika will relay all submissions to the HRC Secretariat.

No later than ten days before the date of review, the HRC Secretariat will transmit any pre-submitted questions and issues to the SuR.

Delegates wishing to make statements during the interactive dialogue may register when the list of speakers opens on the previous working day.

SuR should meet with the troika for better co-ordination and preparation of the Review.

WORKING GROUP SESSION

Interactive dialogue

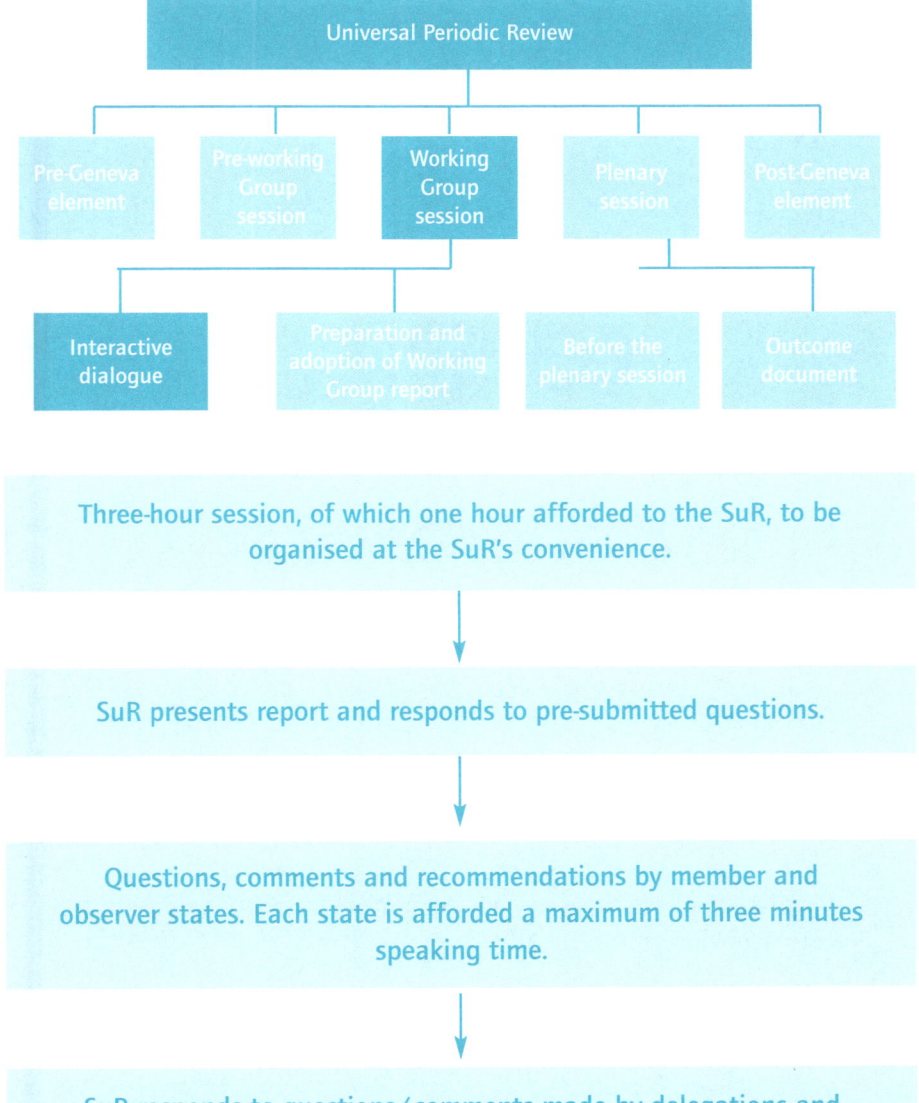

Universal Periodic Review

- Pre-Geneva element
- Pre-working Group session
- **Working Group session**
- Plenary session
- Post-Geneva element

Working Group session:
- **Interactive dialogue**
- Preparation and adoption of Working Group report

Plenary session:
- Before the plenary session
- Outcome document

Three-hour session, of which one hour afforded to the SuR, to be organised at the SuR's convenience.

↓

SuR presents report and responds to pre-submitted questions.

↓

Questions, comments and recommendations by member and observer states. Each state is afforded a maximum of three minutes speaking time.

↓

SuR responds to questions/comments made by delegations and makes concluding comments.

The state is sovereign in addressing the questions/issues it chooses to answer during the interactive dialogue.

WORKING GROUP SESSION

Preparation and adoption of Working Group report

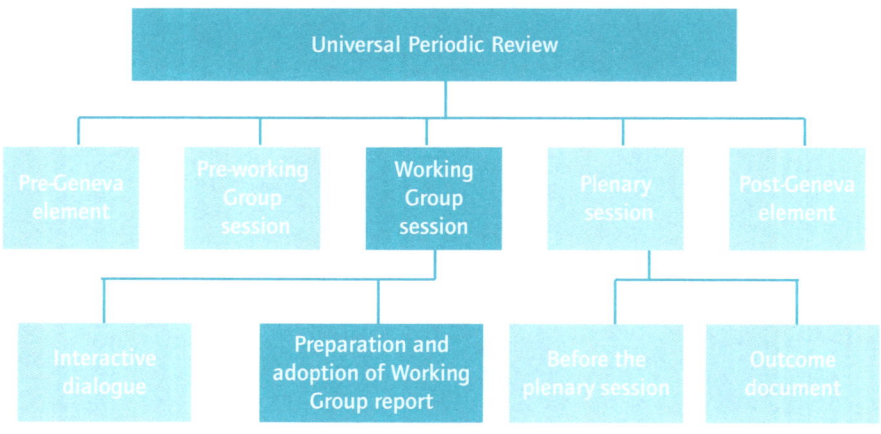

Preparation of Working Group report facilitated by the troika, with the full involvement of the SuR, with the assistance of the HRC Secretariat.

The factual report is made up of:

Part I: Summary of interactive dialogue

Part II: List of conclusions and recommendations made during the course of the interactive dialogue

(on the 2nd day after the interactive dialogue)

30-minute session

Adoption of the Working Group by the HRC

PLENARY SESSION – held during a regular session of the HRC

Before the plenary session

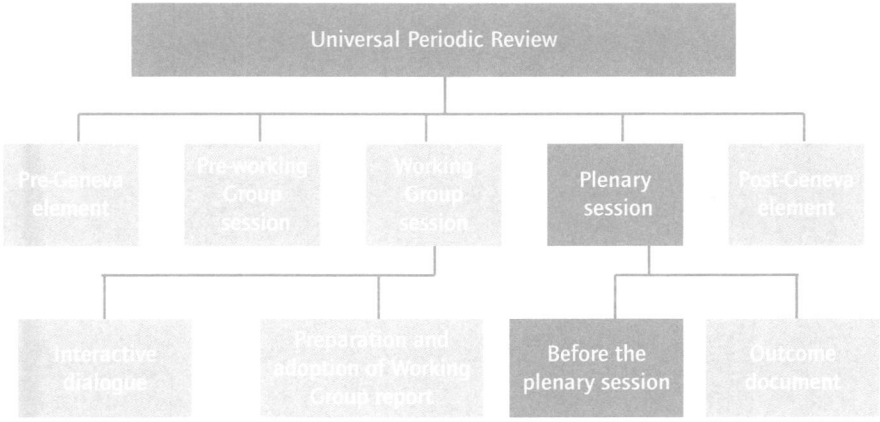

Delegates and stakeholders wishing to make statements during the interactive dialogue may register when the list of speakers opens on the previous working day.

Consideration of the outcome

One-hour session

Statement of SuR (20 minutes maximum)
SuR presents, as appropriate:

- Further views concerning recommendations, conclusions or any voluntary pledges
- Reply to questions not sufficiently addressed during the Working Group session
- Make final comments

Statements on outcome by member states, observer states and UN agencies (20 minutes maximum: 3 minutes per member state, 2 minutes per observer state, 2 minutes per UN agency).

General comments made by stakeholders (NHRI/CSOs) (20 minutes maximum, two minutes per speaker).

Concluding remarks by SuR.

PLENARY SESSION

Outcome document

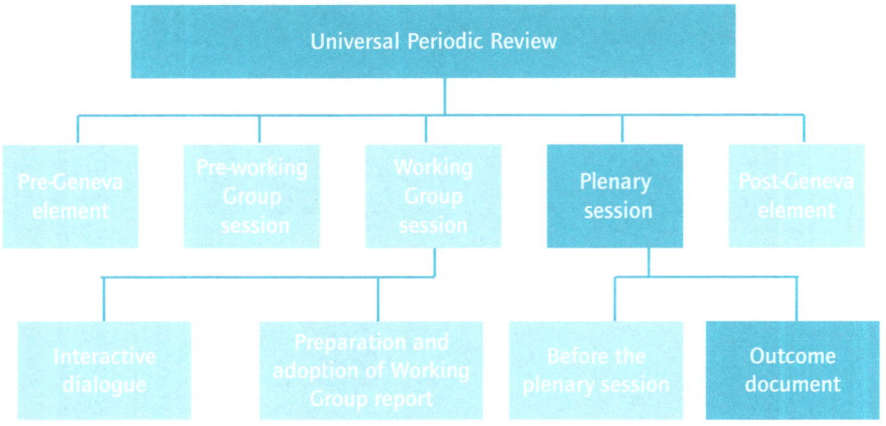

Part I: Summary of proceedings of review process at:

- Working Group level
- Plenary level

Part II: Conclusions and/or recommendations:

- Recommendations that enjoy the support of SuR
- Other recommendations noted with comments of SuR

Part III: If appropriate, voluntary commitments/pledges by SuR

Post-Geneva element

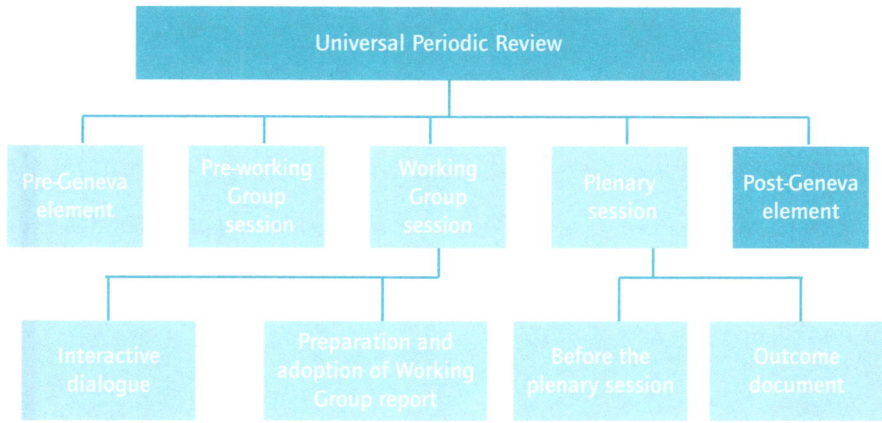

State and stakeholders encouraged to continue dialogue and consultations into the implementation phase of accepted recommendations.

States and stakeholders should widely disseminate information on recommendations and voluntary pledges, if any, to the public.

States and stakeholders to agree programme of action on how best to implement the recommendations.

States, with stakeholders, to begin preparing for the next round of review in four years time incorporating review/evaluation of implementation during that period.

Annex 4

Trust Funds*

Human Rights Council

VOLUNTARY FUND FOR PARTICIPATION IN THE UNIVERSAL PERIODIC REVIEW MECHANISM

Pursuant to resolution 6/17 of the Human Rights Council, a Trust Fund is established by the Secretary-General of the United Nations to facilitate the participation of developing countries, and in particular the least developed countries, in the Universal Periodic Review (UPR)

I. Purpose

The UPR is a mechanism of the Human Rights Council for reviewing, on a regular basis, the fulfilment by United Nations Member States of their human rights obligations and commitments. All 192 United Nations Member States are to be reviewed within a period of four years in the first cycle – with 48 States to be reviewed every year.

The Review is carried out, with the full involvement and in the presence of the State under consideration, by a working group composed of members of the Council that meets three times per year for two weeks and is facilitated by groups of three States members of the Council which will act as Rapporteurs (or 'troikas') appointed by the Council. The UPR Mechanism should not be overly burdensome for the concerned State.

The Voluntary Trust Fund for Participation in the UPR Mechanism is established as a financial mechanism to provide:

i. funding for the travel of official representatives of developing countries, and in particular the least developed countries, to Geneva to present the national report, take part in the ensuing inter-active dialogue and be involved in the adoption of the report in the UPR Working Group sessions during which their country is considered; and

ii. funding for the travel of official representatives of developing countries, and in particular the least developed countries which are members of the Human

---

*UN document. Please see: http://www.upr-info.org/IMG/pdf/TRUST_20FUND_E.pdf

Rights Council and which do not have a permanent mission in Geneva, to act as Rapporteur (i.e. member of the 'troika'):

iii. training for Member States in the preparation of national reports.

II. Application for Financial Assistance

Financial assistance from the Fund may be requested by any developing country, in particular the least developed countries, which are Members of the United Nations.

A. Travel

Reimbursement of travel expenses to attend the meetings of the UPR Working Group under point I (I) and (ii) above, will cover:

1. one round-trip economy class ticket per delegation for a representative not residing in Geneva;

2. three days of Daily Subsistence Allowance (DSA) at the Geneva rate at the time of the meeting, in order to enable one representative not residing in Geneva to participate in the adoption of the report of the UPR Working Group following the review.

Requests for financial assistance should be submitted, at the latest, six weeks before the beginning of the UPR Working Group session to which the representative will be traveling.

Subject to the availability of funds, confirmation of approval will be returned with an indication of the maximum ticket cost to be reimbursed, in accordance with the applicable United Nations rules and procedures for official travel. *Exceptionally, for the first and second sessions of the UPR Working Group, the Secretariat will accept requests for financial assistance during the session.*

Reimbursement of travel expenses will be made by the United Nations after completion of such travel and on receipt of a claim with supporting documentation, within the above-mentioned conditions, directly to the Government concerned, normally through the permanent mission in Geneva or New York.

B. Training in the preparation of reports

Requests for training shall be accompanied by:

1. a detailed description of the proposed training course for the preparation of national reports;

2. information on training arrangements, including location, facilities, logistical aspects, number and position of trainees;

3. an itemized statement of the estimated costs for which assistance is requested, including costs for travel of OHCHR staff, if applicable.

III. Funding and Disbursements

Contributions to the Fund are made voluntarily by States, intergovernmental and non-governmental organizations or private institutions and individuals.

Disbursements are subject to the availability of funds.

In case financial resources are insufficient to cover all requests for financial assistance, the following priorities will apply:

a. requests for travel will be given priority over requests for training;

b. requests for financial assistance for travel to UPR Working Group sessions from least developed countries will be given priority over requests from other developing countries;

c. requests for financial assistance to present the national report, take part in the ensuing interactive dialogue and be involved in the adoption of the report in the UPR Working Group will be given priority over requests to take part in the Working Group sessions as Rapporteurs ('troika member');

d. order of receipt of requests for financial assistance.

Annex 5

Information and Guidelines for Stakeholders[1] on the UPR Mechanism*
[as of July 2008]

I. BACKGROUND

1. The Universal Periodic Review (UPR), established by General Assembly resolution 60/251 of 15 March 2006, is a new human rights mechanism. Through the UPR, the Human Rights Council (HRC) reviews, on a periodic basis, the fulfillment by each of the United Nations' 192 Member States of their human rights obligations and commitments. Resolution 60/251 provides that the UPR shall;[2]

- Be based on objective and reliable information of the fulfillment by each State of its human rights obligations and commitments;

- Be conducted in a manner which ensures universality of coverage and equal treatment with respect to all States;

- Be a cooperative mechanism, based on an interactive dialogue, with the full involvement of the country concerned and with consideration given to its capacity-building needs; and

- Complement and not duplicate the work of treaty bodies.

2. HRC resolution 5/1 of 18 June 2007 provides that the UPR should 'ensure the participation of all relevant stakeholders, including non-governmental organizations and national human rights institutions, in accordance with General Assembly resolution 60/251 of 15 March 2006 and Economic and Social Council resolution 1996/31 of 25 July 1996, as well as any decisions that the Council may take in this regard'.[3]

II. BASIS OF THE REVIEW

3. States are reviewed on the basis of:[4]

The Charter of the UN;

The Universal Declaration of Human Rights;

Human rights instruments to which the State is party;

---

*UN document. Please see: http://www.ohchr.org/EN/HRBodies/UPR/Documents/Technical GuideEN.pdf

Voluntary pledges and commitments, including (where relevant) those undertaken when presenting candidature for election to the HRC; and

Applicable international humanitarian law.

III. UNIVERSAL PERIODIC REVIEW AS A PROCESS

4. Reviewing all 192 UN Member States over a four-year cycle, the UPR is to be seen as a process consisting of several steps:

- Preparation of the information upon which reviews are based, including: (i) information prepared by the State under review (national report); (ii) a compilation of UN information on the State under review prepared by the OHCHR, and (iii) a summary of information submitted by other relevant stakeholders, also prepared by OHCHR. The UPR review is based on these three documents, all of which are public;

- The review itself takes place in Geneva in the Working Group on the UPR, composed of the 47 Member States of the HRC, and takes the form of an interactive dialogue held between the State under review and the Member and Observer States of the HRC. The Working Group meets in three two-week sessions each year and reviews 16 States at each session – a total of 48 States each year;

- The Working Group's adoption of an outcome document at the end of each review;

- The HRC's consideration and adoption of the UPR outcome, normally at the next regular HRC session; and

- Follow-up by reviewed States on the implementation of the conclusions and recommendations contained within outcome documents.

5. The participation of all relevant stakeholders is encouraged throughout all relevant steps of the process. According to Human Rights Council resolution 5/1 of 18 June 2007:

   (a) States are encouraged to prepare the information they submit 'through a broad consultation process at the national level with all relevant stakeholders' (paragraph 15 (a));

   (b) Other relevant stakeholders may submit additional, credible and reliable information to the universal periodic review. Input received from stakeholders will be summarized by the Office of the High Commissioner for Human Rights in a Summary of Stakeholders' information which shall not exceed 10 pages (paragraph 15 (c));

(c) Other relevant stakeholders may attend the review in the working group (paragraph. 18 (c)), while not taking active part in the interactive dialogue;

(d) Before the adoption of the outcome by the plenary of the Council, the State concerned is offered the opportunity to present replies to questions or issues; Other relevant stakeholders will have the opportunity to make general comments before the adoption of the outcome by the plenary (paragraphs 29 and 31);

(e) The outcome of the universal periodic review, as a cooperative mechanism, should be implemented primarily by the State concerned and, as appropriate, by other relevant stakeholders (paragraph 33).

IV. CONTRIBUTING WRITTEN SUBMISSIONS TOWARDS THE UPR PROCESS

A. Documentation upon which reviews are based

6. The documents on which reviews are based are:[5]

    (a) Information prepared by the State concerned, which can take the form of a national report, on the basis of General Guidelines adopted by the HRC at its sixth session, and any other information considered relevant by the State concerned, which could be presented either orally or in writing, provided that the written presentation summarizing the information will not exceed 20 pages.

    (b) A compilation prepared by OHCHR of the information contained in the reports of treaty bodies, special procedures, including observations and comments by the State concerned, and other relevant official UN documents, which shall not exceed 10 pages.

    (c) Additional, credible and reliable information provided by other relevant stakeholders to the UPR which should also be taken into consideration by the HRC in the review. OHCHR will prepare a summary of such information which shall not exceed 10 pages.

B. Content and format of written submissions by relevant stakeholders to the OHCHR

7. HRC decision 6/102[6] sets out General Guidelines for the preparation of information under the UPR. These Guidelines (available at http://ap.ohchr.org/documents/sdpage_e.aspx?b=10&se=69&t=3) apply to States and other stakeholders, as well as to OHCHR for the preparation of the documents under its responsibility.[7]

8   Drawing from the above-mentioned general guidelines, stakeholders may wish to include in their submissions:

(a) The methodology and the broad consultation process followed nationally for the preparation of information provided to the UPR by the country under review;

(b) The current normative and institutional framework of the country under review for the promotion and protection of human rights: constitution, legislation, policy measures such as national action plans, national jurisprudence, human rights infrastructure including national human rights institutions ... ;

(c) The implementation and efficiency of the normative and institutional framework for the promotion and protection of human rights as described at subparagraph (b) above. This includes information on the implementation of the country's human rights obligations and commitments at the national and the international levels (for example information on the implementation of commitments made by the country under review at international conferences and other United Nations fora; of constitutional and legal reforms aimed at protecting human rights, of national action plans, of mechanisms and remedies aimed at improving human rights); on the activities of national human rights institutions; on human rights education and public awareness ... ;

(d) Cooperation of the country under review with human rights mechanisms, and with national human rights institutions, NGOs, rights holders, human rights defenders, and other relevant national human rights stakeholders, both at the national, regional and international levels;

(e) Achievements made by the country under review, best practices which have emerged, and challenges and constraints faced by the country under review;

(f) Key national priorities as identified by stakeholders, initiatives and commitments that the State concerned should undertake, in the view of stakeholders, to overcome these challenges and constraints and improve human rights situations on the ground. This includes, for example, national strategies, areas where further progress is required, steps regarding implementation and follow-up to recommendations made by human rights mechanisms, commitments for future cooperation with OHCHR and human rights mechanisms and agencies, etc.;

(g) Expectations in terms of capacity-building and technical assistance provided and/or recommended by stakeholders through bilateral, regional and international cooperation.

9. Stakeholders are strongly encouraged to provide written submissions that:

- Are specifically tailored for the UPR;

- Contain credible and reliable information on the State under review;

- Highlight the main issues of concern and identify possible recommendations and/or best practices;

- Cover a maximum four-year time period;

- Do not contain language manifestly abusive;

- Are no longer than five pages in the case of individual submissions, to which additional documentation can be annexed for reference. Submissions by large coalitions of stakeholders can be up to ten pages.

10. Stakeholders are encouraged, while drafting their contribution, in accordance with Human Rights Council resolution 5/1 (paragraph 1), to take into consideration all human rights obligations and commitments, including those set out in the United Nations Charter, the Universal Declaration of Human Rights, Human Rights instruments to which the country under review is a party, voluntary pledges and commitments made by that country, as well as applicable international humanitarian law.

11. Stakeholders may also, if they so wish, draw attention to specific conclusions and recommendations made by international and regional human rights mechanisms, and refer to the extent of implementation. However, stakeholders should refrain from listing all treaties ratification, concluding observations and recommendations of the human rights treaty bodies and/or the special procedures of the HRC, as the latter are reflected in the UN compilation prepared by OHCHR.

12. The UPR mechanism does not provide for confidentiality and is conducted on the basis of public documents. Submissions, as originally received, will be made available on-line on OHCHR's website, including the name of the submitting party (provided they do not contain language manifestly abusive).

13. Stakeholders are encouraged to consult with one another at the national level for the preparation of the UPR submissions. Joint submissions by a large number of stakeholders are encouraged. **For detailed technical guidance on modalities for stakeholders' submissions please refer to the information box annexed to these guidelines.**

C. How and when should relevant stakeholders submit information?

14. Stakeholders' submissions should be sent to uprsubmissions@ohchr.org.

15. Deadlines for stakeholders' submissions can be found here at http://www.ohchr.org/EN/HRBodies/UPR/Pages/NewDeadlines.aspx

17. For future country reviews under the UPR, stakeholders should note that written submissions to OHCHR should be sent indicatively at least five months before the relevant session of the Working Group on UPR, to take into account UN Conference Services' requirements. The exact deadlines will be posted in due course on the website.

V. PARTICIPATION IN THE UNIVERSAL PERIODIC REVIEW

18. NGOs in consultative relationship with ECOSOC may attend sessions of the Working Group on the UPR.[8] At these sessions there is no provision for such NGOs to take the floor or submit written information;

19. NGOs in consultative relationship with ECOSOC may participate in regular sessions of the HRC, at which UPR outcomes are considered and adopted, and make brief general comments before the adoption of outcome documents by the HRC.[9]

   For information on how to be accredited to HRC sessions please visit http://www2.ohchr.org/english/bodies/hrcouncil/.

VI. FOLLOW-UP TO THE UNIVERSAL PERIODIC REVIEW

20. Relevant stakeholders may wish to contribute to the follow-up to the outcome of the UPR process, to the extent that this is appropriate:

   (a) Follow-up action could be undertaken in cooperation with the State entities, to whom the recommendations are addressed; and

   (b) Stakeholders may disseminate the outcome of the UPR at the national level.

21. Stakeholders are encouraged to further disseminate these guidelines and raise awareness on the UPR.

VII. CONTACT INFORMATION

22. For further information, please contact:
   OHCHR Civil Society Unit
   Tel: +41 22 917 96 56
   Fax: +41 22 917 90 11
   E-mail: civilsocietyunit@ohchr.org

Technical guidelines for the submission of stakeholders' information to OHCHR

Where to submit?

Written information for the UPR review should be sent to the following address: uprsubmissions@ohchr.org. Please avoid sending information to other OHCHR electronic addresses. Please note (a) the OHCHR secretariat will confirm electronically receipt of your message and submission; and (b) while stakeholders are discouraged to fax or mail a hardcopy of their submission to the OHCHR secretariat, they may do so in the case of repeated technical difficulties with electronic mail to: +41 22 917 90 11.

Format of the written submission:

- Each electronic submission and relevant e-mail message should refer to **one country only**. In the **e-mail message** accompanying the submitted documents kindly include:

- In the title of the e-mail message: the name of the (main) stakeholder/ NGO submitting the contribution, the kind of contribution (individual and/or joint), the name of the reviewed country and indicate the month and year of relevant UPR session, e.g. *'Women's coalition – joint UPR submission – Brazil – April 2008'*;

- In the text of the e-mail message accompanying the submission, stakeholders should indicate the details of the relevant contact person;

- A paragraph describing the main activities of the submitting organization/ coalition, as well as date of establishment, especially for those organizations which interrelate for the first time with the UN, would be also welcomed;

- Should the submission be prepared jointly, the names of all submitting stakeholders should appear at the beginning of the submission text (not in the relevant e-mail message).

- Stakeholders' submissions should not be longer than five pages, to which a more detailed and factual report maybe attached; submissions by large coalitions of stakeholders can be up to ten pages;

- Written submissions should be saved as a Word document only, i.e. not as PDF file, in Times New Roman, font 12;

- Written contributions should be submitted in UN official languages only, preferably in English, French or Spanish;

- Written submissions should be final; in principle, it will not be possible to accommodate revisions;

- Paragraphs and pages of each submission should be numbered;

- Stakeholders are encouraged to include in their written submissions an introductory executive summary, capturing the main points contained therein; as a way of introduction, key words may also be indicated (e.g. domestic violence);

- Written submissions should not include second-hand information (except when it clearly supports original information). Facts and details to support the identified priority issues and recommendations may be annexed for reference to the submission;

- Annexes to the submissions should NOT include pictures, maps, organizations' annual reports or reports from other organizations;

- OHCHR's summary will not refer to names of individuals mentioned in the written submission, except if they refer to emblematic cases;

- The extensive use of footnotes is discouraged;

Please note also:

- Submissions in excess of the five/ten page maximum will not be considered;

- Submissions received in a language other than the six official UN languages will not be considered;

- Submissions received after specified deadlines will not be considered; and

- Submissions containing language manifestly abusive (i.e. incitement to violence, inherently racist language, etc.) will not be considered.

Notes

1 Stakeholders, which are referred to in resolution 5/1, include, inter alia, NGOs, national human rights institutions, human rights defenders, academic institutions and research institutes and regional organizations, as well as civil society representatives.
2 See operative paragraph (op.) 5(e).
3 See para 3(m) of the Annex to resolution 5/1.
4 See para 1 of the Annex to resolution 5/1.
5 See para 15 of the Annex to resolution 5/1.
6 Of 27 September 2007.
7 See section I, 'General guidelines for the preparation of information under the Universal Periodic Review' of HRC decision 6/102.
8 See para. 18(c) of the Annex to resolution 5/1.
9 See para. 31 of the Annex to resolution 5/1.

Annex 6

Different Methodologies Used by Commonwealth Countries in their National Consultation Processes

Listed below are methodologies used by Commonwealth countries that were subject to the UPR process in 2008. The following information is taken from the national report that was presented to the UPR working group session in Geneva.

United Kingdom

All the major Departments of State in the United Kingdom, and the devolved administrations in Scotland, Wales and Northern Ireland, the UK Crown Dependencies and the UK Overseas Territories have been involved in the drafting of the report. In the process of producing the report, the United Kingdom Government has formally consulted the two established national human rights institutions, a range of non-governmental organisations active in the promotion of human rights, and members of civil society who are experts in human rights. Consultation took place at an early stage of drafting, and again before the report was finalised.

India

All concerned Ministries and Departments of the Government of India contributed in the preparation of the report, along with other stakeholders, including the national and state human rights institutions and non-governmental organisations working in the field of human rights and related aspects. Several meetings were held involving the Ministry of Home Affairs, the Ministry of Social Justice and Empowerment, the Ministry of Minority Affairs, the Ministry of Consumer Affairs, Food and Public Distribution, the Ministry of Health and Family Welfare, the Ministry of Housing and Urban Poverty Alleviation, the Ministry of Human Resource Development, the Ministry of Labour and Employment, the Ministry of Law and Justice, the Ministry of Panchayati Raj, the Ministry of Rural Development, the Ministry of Statistics and Programme Implementation, the Ministry of Tribal Affairs, and the Ministry of Women and Child Development. Several consultations were held with the National Human Rights Commission.

A broad consultation process was also held with the stakeholders consisting of several non-governmental organisations involved in human rights related activities along with Ministries in the Government of India. A liberal exchange of views, suggestions and information regarding protection and implementation of human rights took place, which helped in evolving the contours of the national report.

The information collated, subsequent to rigorous and long process of consultations between the Ministries, the national human rights institutions and the non-governmental organisations were used to draft the national report. The report thus evolved, reflects the broad consultative process that was undertaken.

Ghana

In drafting the report, Ministries, Departments, and Agencies of Government, which deal directly or indirectly with human rights, were actively involved in the consultative process. Independent professional associations and bodies, as well as independent human rights institutions where also consulted. These institutions and bodies include, National African Peer Review Mechanism Governing Council, the Ghana Bar Association (GBA), the Ghana Journalist Association (GJA), and the Commission on Human Rights and Administrative Justice (CHRAJ). The consultative process also involved several civil society organizations such as Ark Foundation, Commonwealth Human Rights Initiative and Amnesty International. The Report was drafted following the UN guidelines and was based on information collated during the entire consultative process.

Pakistan

The report was compiled after extensive inter-Ministerial consultations at federal and provincial levels. The Minister for Human Rights held consultations on the draft with noted national NGOs including Save the Children, SEHER, CARITAS, Global Welfare Trust, Research Society of International Law (RSIL) and Ansar Burney Trust.

Zambia

The National Report on the Universal Periodic Review was prepared by the Government of the Republic of Zambia through the Ministry of Justice. Gazette Notice No. 543 of 2003 mandates the Ministry of Justice to deal with matters related to human rights and governance. The Ministry appointed an inter-ministerial committee on human rights comprising relevant ministries and departments, the Judiciary, and Human Rights Commission whose mandate was to coordinate the preparation of the report. Among its tasks the Committee ensured that national consultation was undertaken and input from stakeholders including Civil Society were incorporated into the draft report and thereafter validated through the same process.

In line with the guidelines of the United Nations Human Rights Council adopted at its Sixth Session in September, 2007, Government held nine consultative workshops in all the nine provinces of Zambia. The purpose of the workshops was to, firstly, familiarise the participants with Zambia's obligations under international human rights law and the Universal Periodic Review and, secondly, to gather information on the situation of human rights for inclusion in the national report. Participants in the provincial workshops were drawn from Government institutions, Civil Society Organisations and the Human Rights Commission. The UPR process was highly publicised in order to raise awareness and assure public participation in the country.

Sri Lanka

The Sri Lanka National Report for the Universal Periodic Review (UPR) was prepared by the Government of Sri Lanka (GoSL) following the General Guidelines for the Preparation of Information under the Universal Periodic Review after broad based consultation and discussion with a wide-range of stakeholders.

The Ministry of Disaster Management and Human Rights (MDM and HR) of the GoSL, the lead government agency tasked with the promotion of and coordination of activities connected with human rights, was responsible for organizing meetings/discussions and maintained a continuous dialogue with government ministries and departments, state agencies including the Human Rights Commission of Sri Lanka (HRCSL), police and armed services and with various civil society actors – including individuals and non-governmental organizations. The national report was drafted based on the seven core human rights treaties to which Sri Lanka is state party. The concluding observations of treaty bodies and the reports of the United Nations special procedures mechanisms were studied by relevant government institutions in order to ascertain the areas where the GoSL has made progress in protecting and promoting human rights and to identify shortcomings.

Tonga

The Ministry of Foreign Affairs in consultation with the Prime Minister's Office was responsible for preparing and coordinating Tonga's national report submitted for periodic review by the Human Rights Council of the United Nations. This national report considers basic human rights and fundamental freedoms and the vulnerable sectors of Tongan Society such as children and women.

Consultation took place within capacity constraints. Briefings and preparatory work were undertaken with government ministries and agencies, including the Tonga Police and the Tonga Defence Services.

Almost all of the 49 civil society organisations that are members of the Civil Society

Forum of Tonga (CSFT), which is funded by the United Nations Development Programme (UNDP), were unaware of the UPR process. In recognition of its on-going commitment to dialogue with civil society the Government met with CSFT and has considered their concerns. The Government has also taken into account a report by the one Tongan civil society organisation contributing to this UPR. The General Secretary of the Tonga Church Leaders Forum and the senior staff of the Life-Line Counselling Service were consulted. Discussions were held with the Chief Justice, the Minister for Justice and Attorney General, the Solicitor-General and the Vice President of the Tongan Law Society. In addition the Tonga Chamber of Commerce was consulted as was the President of the Tonga Media Council Inc.

Botswana

The Ministry of Foreign Affairs and International Cooperation was responsible for coordinating an inter ministerial effort towards the preparation of the national report submitted for periodic review by the Human Rights Council of the United Nations. The report was prepared jointly with the Office of the President/Ministry of Justice, Defence and Security and the Attorney General's Office (which comprised the Drafting Committee). Once a draft had been prepared the draft was shared with stakeholder government departments and ministries.

A working draft was then prepared by the Drafting Committee and was shared with stakeholder Government Ministries and Departments with a view that they provide further contribution and feedback. A stakeholder workshop was then convened on 5–6 August 2008 that brought together all stakeholders including the civil society and non-government organizations (NGOs) to go through the initial draft and make comments, suggestions and recommendations to improve the document.

The Bahamas

The Government of The Bahamas has fulfilled its pledge to involve civil society in aspects of human rights promotion. This draft report was forwarded to recognized human rights organizations in The Bahamas prior to its submission to the United Nations Human Rights Council. Regrettably, time constraints have not permitted for the feedback received from human rights organizations to be integrated into this report.

The Government of The Bahamas realizes the imperative of civil society's participation in the development of an amicable human rights environment in The Bahamas. Hence, the Government, by way of its Ministries and agencies, has consulted with various civil society groups in relation to the status of the human rights environment in The Bahamas. With respect to this State report, consultations are ongoing.

Barbados

The national report of Barbados for the Universal Periodic Review was prepared in accordance with the General Guidelines for the Preparation of Information under the Universal Periodic Review.

The Ministry of Foreign Affairs was responsible for coordinating meetings with relevant Government Ministries, NGO's and civil society and the production of the final report. An initial meeting was convened with the principal ministries and government departments responsible for the implementation of the various human rights conventions along with the Office of the Ombudsman. Written submissions were received from those ministries as well as from the National Organization of Women (NOW) and the Barbados Association of Non-Governmental Organizations (BANGO). The submissions and other relevant information were collated into a draft report which was circulated. Further meetings were convened to allow representatives of all the participating agencies as well as NGO's to undertake a thorough review of the draft document. The final report takes into account the results of that review.

Tuvalu

The Department of Foreign Affairs and Labour in consultation with the Office of the Prime Minister and under the guidance of the Government appointed UPR National Task Force, was charged with the responsibility of initiating and coordinating consultations among government stakeholders and the civil society for the Tuvalu national report for the Universal Periodic Review. This national report was written based on the general guidelines adopted by the Human Rights Council in its resolution 5/1 on 18 June 2006. The report considers basic human rights and fundamental freedoms and the vulnerable sectors of the Tuvalu society, and also reviews the human rights implications of the adverse impacts of climate change in particular sea level rise.

Consultations took place within severe capacity constraints. With the assistance from the United Nations Human Rights Office for the Pacific Region based in Fiji Islands, and close consultations with the Office of the Attorney General, the Department of Foreign Affairs and Labour was able to initiate consultations and prepare the national report.

There are more than 45 non-governmental organizations in Tuvalu and not all are aware of the Universal Periodic Review. Consultations were carried out between government stakeholders and the civil society in order to brief them on what the UPR is all about and what human rights issues are for Tuvalu. Briefings and consultations were also done and undertaken within government ministries and departments.

Annex 7

Ratifications of and Signatures to Key Human Rights Treaties by Commonwealth Countries in 2008

Ratifications

International Covenant on Civil and Political Rights (ICCPR)

Country	Date of ratification	UPR session
The Bahamas	23 December 2008	3rd session (2008)
Papua New Guinea	21 July 2008	11th session (2011)
Samoa	15 February 2008	11th session (2011)
Vanuatu	21 November 2008	5th session (2009)
Pakistan	17 April 2008	2nd session (2008)

International Covenant on Economic, Social and Cultural Rights (ICESCR)

Country	Date of ratification	UPR session
The Bahamas	23 December 2008	3rd session (2008)
Pakistan	17 April 2008	2nd session (2008)
Papua New Guinea	21 July 2008	11th session (2011)

Migrant Workers Convention (MWC)

Country	Date of ratification	UPR session
Jamaica	25 September 2008	9th session (2010)

Convention on the Rights of Persons with Disabilities (CRPD)

Country	Date of ratification	UPR session
Australia	17 July 2008	10th session (2011)
Kenya	19 May 2008	8th session (2010)
Lesotho	2 December 2008	8th session (2010)
Uganda	25 September 2008	12th session (2011)
Vanuatu	23 October 2008	5th session (2009)
Cameroon	1 October 2008	4th session (2009)
Malaysia	8 April 2008	4th session (2009)

CRPD Optional Protocol (OP)

Country	Date of ratification	UPR session
Bangladesh	12 May 2008	4th session (2009)
Uganda	25 September 2008	12th session (2011)
Cameroon	1 October 2008	4th session (2009)
Tanzania	29 September 2008	12th session (2011)
Zambia	29 September 2008	2nd session (2008)

Convention on the Elimination of all Forms of Discrimination Against Women (CEDAW), Optional Protocol

Country	Date of ratification	UPR session
Australia	4 December 2008	10th session (2011)

Convention on the Rights of the Child (CRC), Optional Protocol I (Children in Armed Conflict)

Country	Date of ratification	UPR session
Singapore	11 December 2008	11th session (2011)

Signatures

Convention Against Torture (CAT)

Country	Date of signature	UPR session
The Bahamas	16 December 2008	3rd session (2008)
Pakistan	17 April 2008	2nd session (2008)

Convention on the Rights of the Child (CRC), Optional Protocol I (Children in Armed Conflict)

Country	Date of signature	UPR session
Cyprus	1 July 2008	6th session (2009)
Pakistan	25 September 2008	2nd session (2008)
Solomon Islands	23 September 2008	11th session (2011)
Zambia	9 May 2008	2nd session (2008)

Convention on the Rights of the Child, Optional Protocol II (Sale of children, child prostitution and child pornography)

Country	Date of signature	UPR session
Zambia	29 September 2008	2nd session (2008)

Annex 8

Composition of Commonwealth Delegations at UPR Sessions in 2008

Listed below are the delegations sent by the Commonwealth SuR to the UPR working group session held in Geneva.

United Kingdom (10 April 2008)

The delegation of the United Kingdom of Great Britain and Northern Ireland was headed by HE Michael Wills MP, Minister of State for Justice, and was composed of 23 members:

HE Peter Gooderham, Permanent Representative of the United Kingdom of Great Britain and Northern Ireland to the United Nations Office at Geneva

Ms Rebecca Sagar, First Secretary, Human Rights, Permanent Mission of the United Kingdom of Great Britain and Northern Ireland to the United Nations Office at Geneva

Ms Kate Jones, Legal Adviser, Permanent Mission of the United Kingdom of Great Britain and Northern Ireland to the United Nations Office at Geneva

Ms Melanie Hopkins, Second Secretary, Human Rights, Permanent Mission of the United Kingdom of Great Britain and Northern Ireland to the United Nations Office at Geneva

Ms Katriona Gaskill, Second Secretary, Human Rights, Permanent Mission of the United Kingdom of Great Britain and Northern Ireland to the United Nations Office at Geneva

Mr Bob Last, Senior Human Rights Adviser, Permanent Mission of the United Kingdom of Great Britain and Northern Ireland to the United Nations Office at Geneva

Ms Denise Regan, Attaché, Permanent Mission of the United Kingdom of Great Britain and Northern Ireland to the United Nations Office at Geneva

Ms Teresa McGrath, Attaché, Permanent Mission of the United Kingdom of Great Britain and Northern Ireland to the United Nations Office at Geneva

Mr Neil Barcoe, Policy Adviser, Borders and Immigration Agency

Mr Alex Passa, Policy Adviser, Home Office

Mr Rod Clarke, Director General, Ministry of Justice

Mr John Kissane, Deputy Head of Human Rights Division, Ministry of Justice

Mr Glenn Preston, Head of Communications, Human Rights Division, Ministry of Justice

Ms Donna Snaith, Communications and Projects Manager, Ministry of Justice

Mr Rob Smith, Chief Press Officer, Ministry of Justice

Ms Serena Hardy, Head of the Rights and Equalities Law Team, Ministry of Justice

Ms Jo Burden, Private Secretary to the Minister for Justice

Mr Gareth Williams, Senior Adviser, Ministry of Defence

Ms Linda Dann, Legal Adviser, Ministry of Defence

Ms Helena Akiwumi, Senior Adviser, Ministry of Defence

Ms Nadine Brown, Policy Adviser, Northern Ireland Office

Ms Susan Hyland, Head of the Human Rights and Good Governance Group, Foreign and Commonwealth Office

Ms Emma Fraser, United Nations Human Rights Policy Officer, Foreign and Commonwealth Office

India (10 April 2008, afternoon)

The delegation of India was headed by HE Mr Swashpawan Singh, Ambassador and Permanent Representative of India to the United Nations Office at Geneva, and was composed of 13 members:

Mr Goolam E Vahanvati, Solicitor General of India

Mr Vivek Katju, Additional Secretary, Ministry of External Affairs dealing with International Organisations

Mrs Anita Choudhary, Additional Secretary in Ministry of Home Affairs

Mr Mohinder Singh Grover, Deputy Permanent Representative of India to the United Nations Office in Geneva

Mr Manjeev Singh Puri, Joint Secretary, United Nations Division dealing with human rights issues, Ministry of External Affairs

Mr Narinder Singh, Joint Secretary and heads the Legal and Treaties Division of the Ministry of External Affairs

Mrs Manjula Krishnan, Economic Advisor in the Ministry of Women and Child Development

Mr Rajiv Chander, Minister (Political and Economic), Permanent Mission of India to the United Nations Office at Geneva

Mr Raj William, Counsellor, Permanent Mission of India to the United Nations Office at Geneva

Mr Nilambuj Sharan, Deputy Secretary, Ministry of Social Justice and Empowerment

Mr Manu Mahawar, First Secretary, Permanent Mission of India to the United Nations Office at Geneva

Ms Paramita Tripathi, Under Secretary, United Nations Division of the Ministry of External Affairs

South Africa (15 April 2008, afternoon)

The delegation of South Africa was headed by HE Ms Glaudine J Mtshali, Ambassador, Permanent Representative of South Africa to the United Nations Office at Geneva, and was composed of:

Mr J Fick (Minister, Department of Home Affairs)

Mr J Kellerman (Political Counsellor, Department of Foreign Affairs)

Ms B Naidoo (Political Counsellor, Department of Foreign Affairs)

Ms S Matlhako (First Secretary Political, Department of Foreign Affairs)

Mr S Qobo (First Secretary, Department of Foreign Affairs)

Ms S Chung (First Secretary, Department of Foreign Affairs)

Ghana (5 May 2008, afternoon)

The delegation of Ghana was headed by HE Mr Joe Ghartey, Minister of Justice and Attorney-General, and was composed of 11 members:

HE Ms Elizabeth Ohene, Minister of State for Education, Science and Sports

Ms Ama Jantuah Banful, Chief State Attorney

Ms Stella Badu, Principal State Attorney

Ms Evelyn Keelson, Senior State Attorney

Ms Angela Asante-Asare, National Coordinator for Protection, Ministry of Manpower, Youth and Employment

Ms Marian Tackie, Director, International Women's Desk, Ministry of Women and Children's Affairs

Mr Joseph Yaw Aboagye, Director PPMAE, Minerals Commission, Ministry of Lands, Forestry and Mines

Mr Richard Quayson, Deputy Commissioner, Commission on Human Rights and Administrative Justice

Ms Mercy Y Amoah, Deputy Permanent Representative, Permanent Mission of Ghana to the United Nations Office at Geneva.

Ms Loretta Asiedu, First Secretary, Permanent Mission of Ghana to the United Nations Office at Geneva

Pakistan (8 May 2008, afternoon)

The delegation of Pakistan was headed by HE Ms Fauzia Wahab, Member of the National Assembly, and was composed of nine members:

Ms Mahreen Bhutto, Member of the National Assembly, Pakistan

Mr Nawabzada Malik Amad Khan, Member of the National Assembly, Pakistan

HE Ambassador Masood Khan, Permanent Representative of Pakistan to the United Nations

Mr Aftab A Khokher, Counsellor, Permanent Mission of Pakistan, Geneva

Mr Marghoob Saleem Butt, First Secretary, Permanent Mission of Pakistan, Geneva

Mr Imran Ahmed Siddiqui, Director, Ministry of Foreign Affairs, Pakistan

Mr Syed Ali Asad Gillani, First Secretary, Permanent Mission of Pakistan, Geneva

Mr Ahmar Ismail, First Secretary, Permanent Mission of Pakistan, Geneva

Mr Zahid Ahmed Khan Jatoi, Assistant Director, Ministry of Foreign Affairs, Pakistan

Zambia (9 May 2008, morning)

The delegation of Zambia was headed by HE Ms Gertrude Imbwae, Permanent Secretary, Ministry of Justice, and was composed of 19 members:

Mr Mathias Daka, Chargé d'Affaires, Permanent Mission of Zambia to United Nations, Geneva

Ms Encyla Sinjela, Counsellor, Permanent Mission of Zambia to United Nations, Geneva

Ms Sindiso N Kankasa, Governance Secretariat

Ms Inonge K Mweene, Ministry of Justice – ILA

Ms Catherine L Phiri, Directorate of Public Prosecutions

Mr Greenwell Lyempe, Immigration Department

Ms Dorothy Zimba, Police Public Complaints Authority

Mr Tsibu Bbuku, Ministry of Health

Ms Annettee Nhekairo, Zambia Law Development Commission

Mr Edward Musona, Judiciary

Ms Lynn MBS Habanji, Ministry of Lands

Mr Teddy Chola, Zambia Prisons Service

Ms Chileshe Kasoma, Ministry of Community Development and Social Services

Mr John Zulu, Ministry of Youth, Sport and Child Development

Mr Danny Zulu, Ministry of Local Government and Housing

Ms Rhoda Mwiinga, Gender in Development Division

Mr Ronald Kaulule, Ministry of Education

Ms Hope N. Chanda, Human Rights Commission

Mr Palan Mulonda, Human Rights Commission

Sri Lanka (13 May 2008, afternoon)

The delegation of Sri Lanka was headed by Hon. Mahinda Samarasinghe, Minister of Disaster Management and Human Rights, and was composed of 17 members:

Hon. CR De Silva, Attorney-General

HE Dr Dayan Jayatilleka, Ambassador/Permanent Representative of Sri Lanka to the United Nations, Geneva

Mr Suhada Gamalath, Secretary, Ministry of Justice and Law Reform

Ms Malkanthi Wickremasinghe, Secretary, Ministry of Constitutional Affairs and National Integration

Mr Mohan Peiris, PC, Legal Advisor, Ministry of Defence

Professor Rajiva Wijesinha, Secretary General, Secretariat for Co-ordinating the Peace Process

Mr WJS Fernando, Deputy Solicitor-General

Mr Yasantha Kodagoda, Deputy Solicitor-General

Mr Asoka Wijetilake, Deputy Inspector-General of Police

Major General. Ms Mohanthi Peiris, Director-General/Legal, Sri Lanka Army

Mr GKD Amarawardena, Additional Secretary, Ministry of Disaster Management and Human Rights

Mr Sisira Mendis, Deputy Inspector-General of Police

Ms Shirani Goonetilleke, Director/Legal, Secretariat for Co-ordinating the Peace Process

Mr Sumedha Ekanayake, Counsellor, Permanent Mission of Sri Lanka to the United Nations, Geneva

Mr OL Ameerajwad, Counsellor, Permanent Mission of Sri Lanka to the United Nations, Geneva

Mr Ravindra Wickremasinghe, Documentation Officer, Permanent Mission of Sri Lanka to the United Nations, Geneva

Dr Subhashinie Punchihetti, Research Assistant, Permanent Mission of Sri Lanka to the United Nations, Geneva.

Tonga (14 May 2008, afternoon)

The delegation of Tonga was headed by HE Mr Sonatane Tu'akinamolahi Taumoepeau Tupou, Minister of Foreign Affairs, Acting Minister of Defence and Acting Governor of Vava'u, and was composed of five members:

HE Ms Fekitamoeloa 'Utoikamanu, Permanent Representative to the United Nations in New York

HE Dr Ngongo Kioa, High Commissioner to the United Kingdom

Mr Viliami Malolo, Deputy Secretary for Foreign Affairs

Ms 'Ainise Odette Tupouohomohema, Assistant Secretary, Ministry for Foreign Affairs

Mr Gerard Winter, Adviser

Botswana (1 Dec 2008, morning)

The delegation of Botswana was headed by Hon. Mr Dikgakgamatso Seretse, Minister for Defence, Justice and Security, and comprised 13 members:

HE Mr Boometswe Mokgothu, Ambassador and Permanent Representative to the United Nations, Geneva

Mr Augustine Makgonatsotlhe, Secretary for Defence, Justice and Security, Office of the President

Ms Dimpho Mogami, Director, Legal Affairs Department, Ministry of Foreign Affairs

Ms Tebatso Menyatso, Deputy Director, Women's Affairs Department

Mr Pule Mphothwe, Assistant Director, Multilateral Department, Ministry of Foreign Affairs

Mr O Rhee Hetanang, Councellor and Head of Chancery, Botswana Mission to the United Nations, Geneva

Mr Hamilton, Mogatusi, Principal Social Worker, Ministry of Local Government

Ms Chandida Thembe, Principal State Counsel, Attorney General's Chambers

Mr Myron Bonang, First Secretary, Botswana Mission to the United Nations, Geneva

Ms Mabedi T Motlhabani, First Secretary, Botswana Mission to the United Nations, Geneva

Ms Kelebogile M Lekaukau, Trade Attaché, Botswana Mission to the United Nations, Geneva

Mr Michael Manowe, Agriculture Attaché, Botswana Mission to the United Nations, Geneva

The Bahamas (1 Dec 2008, afternoon)

The delegation of Bahamas comprised six members:

Senator the Hon. Michael Barnett, Attorney-General and Minister of Legal Affairs, Head of Delegation

HE Ambassador Joshua Sears, Director-General, Ministry of Foreign Affairs

HE Vernon Burrows, Ambassador, Ministry of Foreign Affairs

Mrs Phedra Rahming, First Assistant Secretary and Officer-in-Charge, Bureau of Women's Affairs, Ministry of Labour and Social Development

Ms Camille Barnett, Adviser

Ms Viola Barnett, Adviser

Barbados (3 Dec 2008, morning)

The delegation of Barbados was headed by HE Christopher Sinckler, MP, Minister of Social Care, Constituency Empowerment, Urban and Rural Development, and comprised 11 members:

HE Ambassador C Trevor Clarke, Permanent Representative to the United Nations and other International Organizations at Geneva

Ms Roslind Jordan-Callender, Principal Crown Counsel, Solicitor General Chambers, Office of the Attorney General

Mr Euclid Goodman, Head of the Multilateral Section, Ministry of Foreign Affairs and Foreign Trade

Mr Joseph Hunte, Human Rights Desk Officer, Ministry of Foreign Affairs and Foreign Trade

Mrs Heather Morris, Senior Administrative Officer, Office of the Attorney General

Dr David Berry, Consultant on International Law

Mrs Emalene Marcus-Burnett, Counsellor, Permanent Mission of Barbados, Geneva

Dr Corlita Babb-Schafer, Counsellor, Permanent Mission of Barbados, Geneva

Mr Matthew Wilson, First Secretary, Permanent Mission of Barbados, Geneva

Ms Natalie Burke, First Secretary, Permanent Mission of Barbados, Geneva

Tuvalu (11 Dec 2008, afternoon)

The delegation of Tuvalu was headed by HE Mr Enele Sopoaga OBE, Permanent Secretary, Department of Foreign Affairs and Labour, and was composed of five members:

Ms Eselealofa Apinelu, Attorney General, Government of Tuvalu

Mrs Manaema Saitala Takashi, Multilateral and International Affairs Officer, Department of Foreign Affairs and Labour, Government of Tuvalu

Mr Seve Lausaveve, Permanent Secretary, Department of Home Affairs

Mrs Imrana Jalal, Human Rights Advisor, Pacific Regional Rights Resource Team

Timetable of Commonwealth Countries Reporting in 2008

	Country	Date of Review	Troika 1	Troika 2	Troika 3
First session	UK	Thursday 10 April (morning)	Egypt Federation	Russian	Bangladesh
	India	Thursday 10 April (afternoon)	Indonesia	Netherlands	Ghana
	South Africa	Tuesday 15 April (afternoon)	Zambia	Guatemala	Qatar
Second session	Ghana	Monday 5 May (afternoon)	Netherlands	Bolivia	Sri Lanka
	Pakistan	Thursday 8 May (afternoon)	Saudi Arabia	Ghana	Azerbaijan
	Zambia	Friday 9 May (morning)	Senegal	Switzerland	Philippines
	Sri Lanka	Tuesday 13 May (afternoon)	Ukraine	Cameroon	Bangladesh
	Tonga	Wednesday 14 May (afternoon)	Nigeria	Qatar	Mexico
Third session	Botswana	Monday 1 December (morning)	Uruguay	Senegal	Slovakia
	The Bahamas	Monday 1 December (afternoon)	Djibouti	Malaysia	Netherlands
	Barbados	Wednesday 3 December (morning)	South Africa	Japan	UK
	Tuvalu	Thursday 11 December (afternoon)	Qatar	Zambia	Azerbaijan

Annex 10

Models Applied by Commonwealth Countries in Responding to Recommendations

Listed below are seven models used by Commonwealth countries in dealing with the conclusions and recommendations of the UPR working group session in Geneva.

The standard pattern is to begin with an introductory sentence, which varies from country to country. For instance, the UK used *'In the course of the discussion, the following recommendations were made to UK'*, and Tonga stated *'The recommendations formulated during the interactive dialogue have been examined by Tonga and the recommendations listed below enjoy the support of Tonga'.*

The introductory sentence is followed by the list of recommendations with a mention of the country or countries that proposed each recommendation, for example:

Expedite ratification of Convention against Torture (Sweden, Italy)

The penultimate sentences consist of different patterns, namely: (a) the SuR could offer immediate comments on the recommendations; (b) the SuR could list recommendations that do not enjoy their support; and (c) the SuR notes the recommendations and offers to provide a response in due time or at the Human Rights Council's regular session. In practice, as stated below, several states have used a combination of these patterns.

The final sentence is a standard note which states: *'All conclusions and/or recommendations contained in the present report reflect the position of the submitting State(s) and/or the State under review thereon. They should not be construed as endorsed by the Working Group as a whole'.*

The **UK**, **Barbados**, **Botswana**, **India** and **South Africa** used the following model:

1. In the course of the discussion, the following recommendations were made to [SuR]

2. The response of [SuR] to these recommendations will be included in the outcome report adopted by the Human Rights Council at its *X* session.

    language used for India: 'These recommendations will be examined by [SuR], which will provide responses in due time. The response of [SuR] will be included in the outcome report to be adopted by the Human Rights Council at its [*X*] session.'

3. All conclusions and/or recommendations contained in the present report reflect the position of the submitting State(s) and/or the State under review thereon. They should not be construed as endorsed by the Working Group as a whole.

Tonga

1. The recommendations formulated during the interactive dialogue have been examined by [SuR] and the recommendations listed below enjoy the support of [SuR]:

   To ratify ... (name of country proposing the recommendation)

   To study ... (name of country proposing the recommendation)

2. The recommendations noted in the report in paragraphs *XX* above did not enjoy the support of [SuR].

3. With regard to recommendations *XX*, the SuR offers the following comments:

4. All conclusions and/or recommendations contained in the present report reflect the position of the submitting State(s) and/or the State under review thereon. They should not be construed as endorsed by the Working Group as a whole.

Pakistan

1. In the course of the discussion, the following recommendations were made to [SuR]:

   To ratify ... (name of country proposing the recommendation)

   To study ... (name of country proposing the recommendation)

2. [SuR] has noted these recommendations for consideration and response in due time. The response of [country] will be included in the outcome report to be adopted by the Human Rights Council at its *X* session.

3. [SuR] considers that other recommendations contained in paragraphs *XX*, *YY* ... cannot be accepted by [SuR].

4. All conclusions and/or recommendations contained in the present report reflect the position of the submitting State(s) and/or the State under review thereon. They should not be construed as endorsed by the Working Group as a whole.

Tuvalu and Zambia

1. The recommendations formulated during the interactive dialogue have been examined by [SuR] and the recommendations listed below enjoy the support of [SuR]:

   To ratify ... (name of country proposing the recommendation)

   To study ... (name of country proposing the recommendation)

2. Recommendations will be examined by [country], which will provide responses in due time. The response of [country] to these recommendations will be included in the outcome report to be adopted by the Council at its X session.

Recommendations noted in paragraphs XX, YY did not enjoy the support of [country].

All conclusions and/or recommendations contained in the present report reflect the position of the submitting State (s) and/or the State under review thereon. They should not be construed as endorsed by the Working Group as a whole.

The Bahamas

1. The recommendations formulated during the interactive dialogue have been examined by [SuR] and the recommendations listed below enjoy the support of [SuR]:

   To ratify ... (name of country proposing the recommendation)

   To study ... (name of country proposing the recommendation)

2. The following recommendations will be examined by [SuR] and the response of the [SuR] to these recommendations will be included in the outcome report adopted by the Human Rights Council at its tenth session

3. Recommendations noted in the report did not enjoy the support of the [SuR]

4. All conclusions and/or recommendations contained in the present report reflect the position of the submitting State (s) and/or the State under review thereon. They should not be construed as endorsed by the Working Group as a whole.

Ghana

1. In the course of the discussion, the following recommendations were made to (SuR).

To ratify ... (name of country proposing the recommendation)

To study ... (name of country proposing the recommendation)

2. The recommendations listed above enjoy the support of [SuR].

3. Recommendations noted in paragraphs *XX, YY,* will be examined by [country] which will provide responses, if any, in due time. Both will be noted in the out-come report to be adopted by the Human Rights Council.

4. All conclusions and/or recommendations contained in the present report reflect the position of the submitting State (s) and/or the State under review thereon. They should not be construed as endorsed by the Working Group as a whole.

Sri Lanka

1. The recommendations formulated during the interactive dialogue have been examined by [SuR] and the following recommendations enjoy the support of [SuR]:

    To ratify ... (name of country proposing the recommendation)

    To study ... (name of country proposing the recommendation)

2. Recommendations noted in paragraphs *XX, YY* ... will be examined by [SuR] which will provide responses in due time. The response of [SuR] will be included in the outcome report to be adopted by the Human Rights Council at its *X* session.

3. Other recommendations noted in the report in paragraphs *XX, YY* ... did not enjoy the support of [SuR].

4. All conclusions and/or recommendations contained in the present report reflect the position of the submitting State (s) and/or the State under review thereon. They should not be construed as endorsed by the Working Group as a whole.

Annex 11

Notes on Contributors

Ms Anna Bossman was appointed Deputy Commissioner in Ghana's Commission on Human Rights and Administrative Justice with overall responsibility for the Legal and Investigations Department. She began her legal career as an Assistant State Attorney at the Ghana Ministry of Justice and Attorney-General's Department and later practised law. She has tutored law students in family law. Ms Bossman is passionate about human rights, with special emphasis on the rights of women and children and environmental issues.

The chapter from the Commonwealth Human Rights Initiative was contributed by **Uttara Sahani** and **Iniyan Ilango**. The CHRI is an independent, non-partisan, international NGO, mandated to ensure the practical realisation of human rights in the countries of the Commonwealth. The CHRI's objectives are to promote awareness of and adherence to the Harare Commonwealth Declaration, the Universal Declaration of Human Rights and other internationally recognised human rights instruments, as well as domestic instruments supporting human rights in Commonwealth member states. It is accredited to the Commonwealth and since 2002 also holds observer status with the African Commission on Human and Peoples' Rights. The CHRI was granted special consultative status with the Economic and Social Council (ECOSOC) of the United Nations in July 2005.

Giuliano Comba heads the Universal Periodic Review Section at the OHCHR, where he is responsible for managing the intergovernmental review process in the UPR working group and the Human Rights Council, as well as overseeing the preparation by the OHCHR of the UPR compilation and stakeholder summary reports which, together with the national reports prepared by states, constitute the basis for the review. Between 1996 and 2005, he was the OHCHR's chief of administration. Since joining the UN system in 1983, he has served as special assistant to the Deputy Executive Director of the United Nations Population Fund (UNFPA), as an assistant administrator of the United Nations Development Programme and as programme manager in both organisations, including UNDP's Bureau for Crisis Prevention and Recovery, on loan from the OHCHR. He has also served as Chief of Administration, World Food Council, and as head of Human Resources Management Information Systems. He began his international career with the European Commission as an administrator of humanitarian and disaster relief programmes in developing countries.

Kieren Fitzpatrick is the foundation director of the Asia Pacific Forum of National Human Rights Institutions (APF), a regional organisation comprised of national human rights institutions from across Asia and the Pacific. He has postgraduate qualifications in law and social science research, and extensive experience in international activities, with a specific focus on social justice and human rights issues.

Cynthia Gervais is the Director of the European Office (in Geneva, Switzerland) of Rights & Democracy (International Centre for Human Rights and Democratic Development). Rights & Democracy is a non-partisan organisation with an international mandate. It was created by Canada's Parliament in 1988 to encourage and support the universal values of human rights and the promotion of democratic institutions and practices around the world. Rights & Democracy's European Office monitors the reform of the UN human rights system, including the work of the Human Rights Council. It has developed and delivered several workshops in relation to this, and particularly on the UPR, both in Geneva and at regional and national level. The objective is to increase the capacity of all stakeholders (civil society, NHRIs and states) to meaningfully participate in, and contribute to, the effectiveness of the UN's human rights mechanisms.

Susan Hyland has been Head of the Human Rights, Democracy and Governance Group in the British Foreign and Commonwealth Office since September 2006. She leads a team of over 20 people, advising on the government's international human rights policy and working through international bodies and other organisations. She is a career diplomat who has served in Paris, Moscow, Oslo and New York. In the UK, she led the team that developed the FCO's first international strategy on human rights. Other recent roles were Chief of Staff to the Head of the Diplomatic Service and head of NATO's arms control teams. Her main areas of interest and expertise include multilateral work and politico-military and trans-Atlantic issues. She has degrees in Philosophy, Politics and Economics (PPE) and in Philosophy from Oxford University. She has also studied at Yale University in the USA and at the French École nationale d'administration.

John Kissane is Deputy Head of the Human Rights Division in the UK Ministry of Justice. He compiled and edited the country UPR report and was project manager for the UK's *Universal Periodic Review* in April 2008. He was also project manager for the UK examinations under the Convention Against Torture in November 2004, and under the International Covenant on Civil and Political Rights in July 2008. He is currently leading on preparations for the UK examination under the International Covenant on Economic, Social and Cultural Rights in May 2009. He is the UK liaison officer for the European Convention for the Prevention of Torture (ECPT).

Viliami Malolo is a former Deputy Secretary for Foreign Affairs, Ministry of Foreign Affairs, Tonga. In this role, he had general responsibility, in co-ordination with other government agencies, for providing policy advice in relation to multilateral institutions such as the United Nations, the Commonwealth Secretariat, the Pacific Islands Forum Secretariat and other institutions of which Tonga is a member. He was also involved in advisory work concerning legal and/or treaty obligations that are of concern to Tonga. He has served on the Tonga Government's Law Reform Committee and is currently a member of the Extended Continental Shelf Committee. He also served as a Deputy National Authorising Officer for the administration of development assistance to Tonga from the European Union. He is currently Tonga's Deputy Permanent Representative at its Permanent Mission to the United Nations in New York.

Ibrahim Salama has been Chief of the Human Rights Treaties Branch at the Office of the United Nations High Commissioner for Human Rights since August 2007. Before that he served as Egypt's ambassador to Portugal (2003–2007) and as Director of the Departments of Legal and Multilateral Legal Affairs of the Ministry of Foreign Affairs, Egypt (2001–2003). He was Egypt's Deputy Permanent Representative to the UN in Geneva (1997–2001) and Director of the Research and Treaty Department of the Ministry of Foreign Affairs (1995–1997). He has also been a member of the UN Sub-Commission on the Promotion and Protection of Human Rights (2004–2008) and served as chairperson of the UN Working Group on the Right to Development (2003–2007). He served as senior adviser on international affairs to the President of the Egyptian Parliament (1995–2003) and was a member of the Egyptian National Committee for the Promotion of International Humanitarian Law (2000–2003). Ambassador Salama holds a PhD in Law from the University of Paris-Sud. He also holds a Diploma in Post-graduate Specialised Studies, DESS, in International Organisations from the University of Paris-Sud and a Diploma in International Political Relations from the International Institute for Public Administration, Paris.

Dr Purna Sen is Head of the Human Rights Unit at the Commonwealth Secretariat. Before joining the Secretariat she was Director of the Asia-Pacific Programme at Amnesty International and previously taught Gender and Development at the Development Studies Institute (DESTIN) at the London School of Economics (LSE). Since the early 1990s, her work has included research, producing publications and activism on violence against women, culture and human rights, particularly in relation to sexual violence, trafficking, civil society organising against violence, as well as social development issues and race equality in the UK. She has worked in a number of countries, including India, Jordan, Morocco and Indonesia, as well as in the Nordic region. She has regional expertise in Asia and the Pacific, and has engaged especially in the conflict areas of Sri Lanka and Nepal, as well as working on human rights issues in Malaysia, Indonesia, Papua New Guinea, Korea and other countries in the region. She has consulted with many organisations, including Article 19 and the British Council. She holds a visiting senior fellowship at DESTIN at the LSE.